THE
REFERENCE
SHELF

ROCK MUSIC IN AMERICA

edited by JANET PODELL

THE REFERENCE SHELF

Volume 58 Number 6

THE H. W. WILSON COMPANY

New York   1987

THE REFERENCE SHELF

The books in this series contain reprints of articles, excerpts from books, and addresses on current issues and social trends in the United States and other countries. There are six separately bound numbers in each volume, all of which are generally published in the same calendar year. One number is a collection of recent speeches; each of the others is devoted to a single subject and gives background information and discussion from various points of view, concluding with a comprehensive bibliography. Books in the series may be purchased individually or on subscription.

Library of Congress Cataloging in Publication Data

Main entry under title:

Rock music in America.

   (The Reference shelf ; v. 58, no. 6)
   Bibliography: p.
   1. Rock music—United States—History and criticism.
I. Podell, Janet. II. Series.
ML3534.R6335   1986   784.5'4'00973   86-32394
ISBN 0-8242-0727-0

Printed in the United States of America

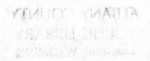

CONTENTS

PREFACE 5

I. THE BIRTH OF ROCK AND ROLL

Editor's Introduction 7
David Evans. Blues and Modern Sound: Past, Present,
    and Future .... Folk Music and Modern Sound   8
Paul Hemphill. Days of Innocence ....
    The Nashville Sound: Bright Lights and Country Music
    17
Linda Ray Pratt. Elvis, or the Ironies of a Southern
    Identity 23
Kurt Loder. The Music That Changed the World ......
    .... Rolling Stone   34

II. ROCK TAKES ROOT

Editor's Introduction 41
Jeff Greenfield. They Changed Rock, Which Changed
    the Culture, Which Changed Us ....
    .... New York Times Magazine   42
Ian Whitcomb. 1966: "The Sounds of Silence" ....
    .... Rock Odyssey   51
Jim McEwen and Jim Miller. Motown ....
    .. The Rolling Stone Illustrated History of Rock & Roll 70
Jim Miller. Some Future .... New Republic   85
Kit Rachlis. Back on the Street Again .... Mother Jones 92
Jay Cocks. Songs from the High Ground .... Time   96

III. THE ROCK MUSIC INDUSTRY

Editor's Introduction 100

Drew Moseley. Jogging for Jovan . Rock Yearbook 1983   101
Ken Barnes. Democratic Radio ....
..........The First Rock & Roll Confidential Report   107
Steven Levy. Ad Nauseam: How MTV Sells Out Rock &
    Roll .... Rolling Stone   120
Steven Dougherty. From 'Race Music' to Heavy Metal:
    A Fiery History of Protests .... People Weekly   143
Pete Townshend. The Punk Meets the Godmother .....
.... Rolling Stone   146

Bibliography 16 4

PREFACE

In American society—a society constantly in motion, continually blending and mixing new elements in a volatile brew—rock music has a unique function. Half art, half big business, it is an immense homogenizer that absorbs the musical traditions and innovations of people separated in every other way—by race, by economic class, by region, by ideology—and recycles them in endless combinations. Easily portable (on radio and records), readily adaptable to other mass art forms such as television and movies, this hybrid music is carried back to its consumers (which includes nearly everybody) in an ongoing process of musical and social cross-fertilization.

The selections in the present volume examine various aspects of this process. They are not intended to constitute a "history" of rock. No attempt has been made to mention all the genres and performers that have come and gone on the rock scene since rock first became a mass phenomenon in the mid-1950s. Important developments such as folk rock, protest songs, rock festivals, reggae, disco, and new wave are touched on only in passing. This book's theme, instead, is the fundamental nature of rock music as the one art form that unites disparate groups of Americans, however imperfectly and unequally. Rock often succeeds in doing what nothing else manages to do: give a divided people a sense that they may have something in common. When both candidates in the 1984 presidential elections invoked rock star Bruce Springsteen in their speeches, they tacitly acknowledged that he was capable of symbolizing certain ideals and hopes for the public in a way that they could not. When rock bands appear among separatist religious groups like the Hasidim, rock can be said to have proved itself adaptable to the needs of virtually every segment of American society. When Paul Simon, a rock star from a "folk rock" background, can persuade his record company to underwrite a collaboration with South African and South American musicians, the cross-fertilization of cultures appears to be reaching global proportions.

But directly or indirectly, African, British, and other musical traditions have been feeding into rock music all along. The first section of this volume, "The Birth of Rock and Roll," focuses on

5

the circumstances under which rhythm and blues, a musical form developed and practiced by the black underclass, was made acceptable to white teenagers under the new name "rock and roll." The flowering of rock as a self-conscious art form with a strong influence on American culture as a whole is examined in the second section, "Rock Takes Root." The last section, "The Rock Music Industry," contains articles on recent developments in how rock music is packaged, marketed, and distributed to the public, as well as a first-hand account of what it's like to suffer the exaltations and punishments of rock stardom.

The editor wishes to thank the authors and publishers who kindly gave permission to reprint the material in this collection. Special thanks are due to Diane Podell of the staff of the B. Davis Schwartz Memorial Library, C. W. Poster Center, Long Island University, and to Jonathan Rogers for his assistance.

JANET PODELL

January 1987

I. THE BIRTH OF ROCK AND ROLL

EDITOR'S INTRODUCTION

The rock and roll era began in 1954, the year when Alan Freed, a Cleveland disk jockey, began playing "race music"—rhythm and blues records made and bought by blacks—for the white teenagers of Middle America. On July 19 of that year, Elvis Presley recorded "That's All Right, Mama," a song by the black blues singer Arthur Crudup. "I knew that there was a big thing here that was basic, that was big, that had to get bigger," recalled concert promoter Hal Zeiger, who was on the scene. "I realized that this music got through to the youngsters because the big beat matched the great rhythms of the human body. I understood that. I knew it and I knew there was nothing anyone could do to knock that out of them. And I further knew that they would carry this with them the rest of their lives."

Throughout its history, rock has owed more to the music produced by the black American community than to any other single source. The evolution of black folk music into new forms—blues, jazz, and ragtime—at the turn of the century, and the transformation of blues into rock and roll a half-century later (as well as its continuing influence on rock performers), is described by ethnomusicologist David Evans in the first selection, "Blues and Modern Sound: Past, Present, and Future," reprinted from the book *Folk Music and Modern Sound*. The other main source of early rock is country music, developed mainly from the folk music of the English immigrants who settled in the Southern mountains. As Evans notes, the first Presley recordings consisted of a blues song on one side and a country song on the other. The contributions of country are discussed in the second selection, "Days of Innocence," an excerpt from Paul Hemphill's book *The Nashville Sound: Bright Lights and Country Music,* which also describes country music's influence on rock star Bob Dylan.

For a detailed reading of Elvis Presley as the apotheosis of Southern culture, as well as the first singer to attempt a unification of black and white musical styles, see Linda Ray Pratt's "Elvis, or the Ironies of a Southern Identity," the third selection.

It is followed by Kurt Loder's *Rolling Stone* article "The Music That Changed the World," about the election of ten rock pioneers, including Presley, to the new Rock and Roll Hall of Fame in 1986—only 32 years after Presley's first hit.

BLUES AND MODERN SOUND: PAST, PRESENT, AND FUTURE[1]

From its very beginnings as a musical form the blues has played a role in popular music and in various manifestations of the "modern sound." It has contributed to popular music at a general level as well as in specific ways to almost every major form and style of American music in the twentieth century. Yet despite these contributions, blues also remains a distinct musical form with its own traditions. Certain performers are still known specifically as "blues singers" or "bluesmen," and many of them perform virtually no other type of music. Such performers have existed throughout the history of the blues. Thus the music has had the peculiar reputation of being something both primitive and modern. Those singers and musicians who specialize in the blues are often considered crude and technically limited by others who perform different musical styles. Many artists state that they can perform blues but do not want to limit themselves to this type of music. Often they view blues as no more than raw material for development and exploitation within other musical styles and traditions.

Admittedly the blues is simple music in respect to its most basic formal characteristics. It uses brief stanza forms and generally no more than three chords in its harmonies, it often employs a pentatonic scale for the melody; and it has texts that frequently seem to skip from one topic to another with little or no logical progression or thematic or narrative unity. In actuality this musical and textual simplicity or crudity is only a superficial characteristic, and blues can be shown to exhibit great subtlety of expression. But this subtlety generally stems from the innate tal-

[1]Excerpted from an essay by David Evans, associate professor of music and director of regional studies in ethnomusicology at Memphis State University. In William Ferris and Mary L. Hart, eds., *Folk Music and Modern Sound.* University Press of Mississippi, '82. Copyright © 1982 by University Press of Mississippi. Reprinted by permission.

ent of composers and performers rather than from their formal
training. The apparent simplicity of the blues probably enables
innate musical talent to be magnified more than in other musical
forms where this talent must be harnessed to more elaborate musical and lyrical structures. Thus the blues is an ideal vehicle of
expression for poor people who have little access to formal musical training. It was among such people that the blues first arose,
and they have continued to pioneer the most creative developments in this music's history. Through blues music many such individuals have been able to find a vehicle of self-expression and
raise themselves temporarily or even permanently out of the rut
of poverty and isolation. It is the purpose of this paper to outline
the contributions of blues to American music in general and to
specific musical forms and traditions and to indicate the present
state and possible future directions of blues both as a self-
contained musical tradition and in relation to the broader spectrum of American music.

In a general sense blues could be considered to have made
major contributions to American music in three areas, namely
scale, form, and subject matter. In fact, each of these characteristics has been used at one time or another to define or characterize
the blues. To our musical scale the blues has contributed the so-
called "blue notes." These have been variously described as flat-
ted notes, neutral pitches, waverings, sliding tones, and tonal
ranges, generally at the third and seventh degrees of the scale but
sometimes at other points as well. However one wants to define
"blue notes," they represent a major breaking away from the European and classical scale. "Blue notes" are pervasive today
throughout virtually all of American popular music as well as that
of many other parts of the world. Actually these notes existed in
earlier forms of Afro-American music such as spirituals and
work-songs and were pointed out by some observers in the nineteenth century, but it was through blues that they spread to other
American musical forms. In fact, through the 1920s the presence
of "blue notes" in a song seems to have been the main criterion
for calling that piece a "blues." Many songs which used ragtime
or popular harmonic progressions and stanza forms were called
"blues" became their scales employed "blue notes."

In respect to musical form the blues has contributed to American music the distinctive three-line AAB stanza pattern with its
familiar harmonic progression. Blues has also contributed certain

two-line and four-line patterns. These patterns have been elabo-
rated in countless ways by many performers and composers, but
their basic outlines are still detectable and can be found throughout popular music. Another important formal characteristic of
blues is the role that the instrument or instruments play in respect
to the singing, namely that of responding to and interacting with
the vocal line. Instruments in the blues do not merely have an accompaniment function but rather represent additional voices.
Their lines are integral parts of the song itself. This elevated role
for instruments within vocal music has now become a standard
feature of American popular music, one that is due to the influence of the blues. These formal characteristics of verse and harmonic pattern and instrumental role are the ones that most
scholars have used to define the blues.

Blues singers themselves generally define the blues as a feeling or an attitude toward life. Basically blues songs avoid senti-
mentality and the idea of progress toward some ideal state of
things. Instead they dramatize and celebrate the ups and downs
of life, enabling singers and their audiences to externalize some
of their strongest feelings, particularly those dealing with inter-
personal relationships between the sexes. Blues contains a realism
and an earthiness that were generally lacking in earlier types of
folk and popular song but which have gradually become more
prevalent in this century in all types of songs.

Blues originated as a distinct type of music shortly before the
beginning of the twentieth century. This was a time of major new
developments in many areas of black music. A new generation
had just reached maturity, born and raised outside the confines
of slavery. This generation broke with the music of the past and
created new forms such as blues, jazz, ragtime, vocal quartet music, folk ballads, and the new music of the Pentecostal churches
featuring the use of a variety of instruments. Out of all of these
musical forms blues probably represented best the music of the
lowest class of black society, the poorest people in the rural areas
of the Deep South, landless sharecroppers and tenant farmers,
hoboes and migratory common laborers, and those who streamed
into the urban slums of the South and the North seeking relief
from oppressive rural social and economic conditions. Blues was
therefore the most "underground" and most "folk" of these new
musical forms and consequently one of the last to be popularized.
In fact, it still retains a strong folk and underground component

with many tradition musical and lyrical elements and many regional, local, and individual stylistic manifestations.

This status can be seen clearly in the reactions of a number of individuals to blues music at the time of its earliest development. Lucius Smith, a ninety-four-year-old banjo player living in Sardis, Mississippi, was already performing string band music for square dancing when blues came on the scene. He didn't like the new music because it was "out of order" and caused people to dance "at random." He associated it with drinking and rowdiness. W. C. Handy, who is often called the "Father of the Blues," actually considered the folk blues to be raw material for popular songs. Handy was a trained musician and could not have composed within a folk blues style, though he had the foresight to recognize good material and incorporate it into his many fine formal compositions. His statements and writings indicate that he was very much aware of the differences between the folk and formal products. J. Mayo Williams, a college educated black man who was a pioneer in the blues recording industry, advertised Blind Lemon Jefferson, the first major folk blues singer to record, in 1926 as "a real old-fashioned blues singer" who sang "old-time tunes" and played guitar "in a real southern style." Many white writers in the late teens and 1920s emphasized the blues' alleged "underworld" associations and unsavory aspects of the songs' subject matter. A similar reaction took place among some whites in the 1950s, when blues once again had significant impact on white popular consciousness. Then the blues was characterized as "jungle music" and its so-called "primitive" aspects pointed out, accompanied by dire warnings about the consequences for white youths who listened or danced to this music.

During its early years blues influenced other emerging popular musical forms. Blues rhythms entered ragtime music, and to some extent the earliest blues compositions on sheet music were simply considered a variety of ragtime music. The blues form and blue notes, however, were foreign to the spirit of ragtime and never were very well incorporated into that musical form. Blues was probably even more at home in early jazz music, as witnessed by the fact that many of the first jazz recording groups featured blues heavily in their repertoires. Blues was also prominent in the repertoires of early vocal quartets like the Norfolk Jazz Quartet and the Birmingham Quartet who began recording in the 1920s. Though blues appeared less in jazz and vocal group music of the

1930s, it made a comeback in bebop music of the 1940s. A large number of the classic bebop pieces of artists like Charlie Parker are actually in the blues form although the harmonies have been greatly altered. Modern jazz has continued to make heavy use of the blues form. The blues also made a strong comeback with vocal groups in the 1950s, although its popularity has since declined in this form of music. Blues has had an important influence on gospel music as well. Thomas A. Dorsey, who is generally considered the father of black gospel music, was a former blues singer, musician, and composer before he entered the gospel field. Blues also seems to have influenced the styles of a number of important pioneer gospel performers such as Blind Willie Johnson, Sister Rosetta Tharpe, and the Staples Singers.

Blues not only influenced other forms of black music, but it has also had a great impact on white music. In fact, it has even influenced the music of some minority ethnic groups in America. Hawaiian music, for example, has incorporated a great number of blues into its repertoire since the 1920s, and there has developed a complex interrelationship between Hawaiian guitar playing and blues slide guitar style. The music of the French-speaking Cajuns of Louisiana has also been heavily influenced by blues in the last few decades, even though the main instruments of accordion and fiddle are unorthodox in black blues tradition.

During the 1920s blues exerted some influence on classical music as seen in the work of composers like George Gershwin. Blues was also very prominent in popular white vaudeville music during this same period. There are many recordings available from the late teens and 1920s of blues by vaudeville artists like Al Bernard, George O'Connor, Cliff Edwards, Marie Cahill, Sophie Tucker, Margaret Young, Dolly Kay, and Marion Harris. The singing was usually rather stiff compared to the work of contemporary black recording artists, but the important thing is that the attempt was being made.

Perhaps the most notable impact of blues on white music has been in the area of country and western music. The man who is often considered to be the first real star of commercial country music, Jimmie Rodgers, rose to fame on the basis of his blue yodels, basically folk blues with yodeling at the ends of some lines and on refrains. Rodgers's popularity resulted in a host of imitators and followers, some of whom are still active in country music. Later on in the 1930s western swing music became quite popular as exemplified by the work of artists like Bob Wills, Milton Brown, and W. Lee O'Daniel, all of whom featured with their bands many blues taken from popular records by black artists. In the 1940s and 1950s the honky tonk style, as exemplified by Hank Williams, utilized many blues tunes. Countless country music stars claim to have been influenced in their formative musical years by black blues performers, and often this influence was direct rather than through records or radio. In the last couple of decades blues seems to have played less of a role in country music, but several recent blues song hits may be indications of a comeback for the blues.

Rock and roll music grew out of a mixing of blues and country music that first took place in the 1950s. This is seen most dramatically in the early work of Elvis Presley and some of his contemporaries who recorded for the Sun Record Company of Memphis. Each of Presley's earliest records contained a blues on one side backed by a country tune. The blues songs were Presley's adaptations of pieces that had recently been popularized by black recording artists. Jerry Lee Lewis, Carl Perkins, Bill Haley, and other early white rock and roll stars also recorded a very high percentage of blues. Their black rock and roll counterparts like Chuck Berry, Fats Domino, Little Richard, and Bo Diddley also recorded a great many blues, while some even more traditional artists like Big Joe Turner and Jimmy Reed had major hits with straight blues pieces. By the early 1960s the role of blues had declined within rock and roll music due to changing popular tastes and a reactionary stance of certain forces within the music industry who found blues to be too earthy. At this time white appreciation for blues shifted to folk music revival circles. Though the folk revival was a somewhat underground movement that produced few popular hits, and hardly any of these being blues, it did expose millions of young whites, including many musicians, to the music of highly traditional folk blues singers like Lightnin' Hopkins, John Lee Hooker, Muddy Waters, Mississippi John Hurt, Big Joe Williams, Son House, and Brownie McGhee and Sonny Terry. Many performers who later enjoyed successful careers in popular music, such as Bob Dylan, came out of the folk revival movement of the early and mid-1960s. Big Joe Williams, in fact, to this day claims to have discovered Bob Dylan, and it is true that some of Dylan's first commercial recordings were as a harmonica player on some Williams tracks that appeared on an album on the

Spivey label. By the later 1960s several white artists from folk revival backgrounds had formed amplified blues bands, and one
group, Canned Heat, even had several big hits with blues tunes.
Meanwhile, British groups like the Beatles, Rolling Stones, and
Yardbirds had been copying the earlier records of Chuck Berry,
Howlin' Wolf, Slim Harpo, Muddy Waters, and other black stars
and making a major impact on young white American audiences.
During the 1970s the blues influence on rock and roll became less
direct, although blues-influenced lead guitar playing became the
norm. Today most rock groups perform a few blues, though few
maintain mass popularity by doing mainly or exclusively blues.
Nevertheless, millions of whites are now familiar with blues and
enjoy it when they hear it though they may prefer it in limited
doses or in diluted form.

Blues has had a continuous history of stylistic development
among blacks throughout this century in addition to influencing
so many other forms of music. In general, this development has
moved in the direction of greater musical sophistication and complexity. There has, however, always been a folk blues tradition.
Folk blues achieved considerable popularity among blacks
through phonograph records in the late 1920s, and while this
popularity declined somewhat in the 1930s, the folk styles by no
means disappeared. In fact, they made a strong comeback on
records and in clubs in the late 1940s and the 1950s. But by the
end of the 1950s blues had begun to decline seriously in popularity among blacks. This slump lasted through the 1970s. Blues received less and less jukebox and radio play. Record companies
began dropping blues artists or else orienting their releases toward the growing white audience for blues. New and younger
blues artists were not recorded and promoted, and the black audience for blues began growing increasingly older and smaller. The
top blues singers of 1980, such as B. B. King, Albert King, Little
Milton, Bobby Bland, Muddy Waters, and John Lee Hooker are
the same ones who were stars in 1960. I think the reason for this
decline in popularity is that blues seemed to many blacks to be in-
consistent with the aims of the Civil Rights movement. Blues
seemed to represent old attitudes and living conditions rather
than progress. It was unsophisticated music and had associations
with the Old South and with an older generation that had learned
to live with segregation. A musical generation gap developed
among blacks from the late 1950s through the 1970s, just as a gap

also developed among whites. But whereas many young whites embraced the blues as their symbol of rebellion, blacks by and large rejected this same music and turned instead to the soul sounds of James Brown, Wilson Pickett, Aretha Franklin, and the Supremes. These artists seemed to capture in their music the spirit of what younger blacks were striving for. Today the blues is definitely a minority musical taste among blacks.

What, then is the future of the blues? Is it destined to fade away and eventually die out as the older artists leave the scene? Will the music be sustained, as some have predicted, only by white musicians? I think not. Instead I detect a serious renewal of interest in blues among young black people. At present this is still largely an underground movement, but within two or three years I predict it will make a major impact on black popular music. Just as a new generation born outside of slavery created the blues, so now a new generation has come to maturity that grew up in the Civil Rights era. Not all of the Civil Rights battles have been won by any means, but the gains that have been made have allowed many people to look back on their historical and cultural past and reassess it. A realization is occurring that the generations who had to live with slavery and segregation did not simply passively accept it but rather remained able to create significant expressions of the human spirit such as the spirituals and the blues. Undoubtedly the recent popular television series and book, *Roots*, by Alex Haley has had much to do with this reassessment of the past. But I think *Roots* simply captured the spirit of a movement that was bound to take place at this time. In fact, a "roots" phenomenon has also been apparent in recent years among young whites, stimulated in part by the recent American Bicentennial. Young members of regional and ethnic groups everywhere are seeking identity in their "roots" and attempting to restore their ties with the past that had been broken during the "generation gap" of the last twenty or more years. Black people too are increasingly looking upon themselves as members of an ethnic group with a distinctive history and cultural tradition, just like other American ethnic groups, and not simply as black Americans who have less of everything that other Americans have because of past and present injustices.

This "roots" phenomenon has manifested itself in the blues in a number of ways that I have been able to observe. Older blues musicians, who ten years ago used to drive young people away in disgust with their music, now report that youngsters are flocking around them trying to learn blues or wanting to form bands with them. Many older and middle aged bluesmen are now starting to train their children in this music and form family bands, now that the "roots" emphasis has made the family tradition something to be highly valued. Outdoor folk festivals, concerts, and television specials on blues have demonstrated to young blacks that there is widespread, even international interest in this music and that there are opportunities for significant monetary income and fame in the blues. . . .

I predict that this roots emphasis will intensify in the next few years with increasing media exposure, festivals, and presentation in the schools. The younger blues players are still mainly working as instrumentalists and generally seem to be a bit shy about singing blues. Perhaps they feel unready to try to match the power of the older singers. But I don't expect it to take long to overcome this hurdle. All the music needs at this point is for one or two attractive and good young performers to get the right media exposure with a good selling record or a major television appearance. This is bound to happen soon, and when it does, I think we will see hundreds of other young blues singers and musicians appearing out of nowhere and trying to get in on the action. I believe that whites will continue to participate in blues but will by no means take the music over. Whites will continue to come to blues from folk revival, rock, and country music backgrounds, but rather than borrow a little from blues and then go off and create some new synthetic style, I believe whites will increasingly participate in blues on black musical terms. In fact, I have noticed that many of the blues bands in Mississippi have one or two white members, and I understand that this has been the case in Chicago for several years. These would appear to be white musicians who have more than a superficial commitment to the blues.

I see the blues finally attaining a status that it has always had but which has not been fully recognized by most Americans, namely that of a distinctive stream within American music with a history and stylistic development of its own as well as an enormous influence on other musical forms in this country and throughout the world. I see a growing parity in this country between folk, popular, and classical styles of music, which will benefit blues in achieving the stature it deserves. I also see an increasing appreciation for innate talent and artistry to the point where they are valued equally with formally developed technical skills. Musicians and their audiences will go beyond the apparent simplicity of the blues form to appreciate the subtleties of expression that can result from innate abilities. The fruits of this new consciousness should be apparent within a few years in a renewed status and popularity for blues music in all segments of American society.

DAYS OF INNOCENCE[2]

A Hill-Billie is a free and untrammelled white citizen of Alabama, who lives in the hills, has no means to speak of, dresses as he can, talks as he pleases, drinks whiskey when he gets it, and fires off his revolver as the fancy takes him.

—The New York *Journal*, April 23, 1900

Well, maybe the New York *Journal* was right when it became the first to use the word "hillbilly." Most likely the hills were in Kentucky or Tennessee or West Virginia rather than in Alabama, and most likely the *Journal*'s man brought a few Yankee biases with him when he came to report this phenomenon from the scene, but you'd really be splitting hairs if you tried to quibble over the description of the nation's most backward citizen at the turn of the century. These were the offspring of the most rugged of the people who had come over from the British Isles on the first boats, and that is damned rugged. Boston and Norfolk and Charleston and Richmond and Philadelphia had been too big for them. There wasn't a city or a town or a village or even a hamlet that could hold them. They were forever cutting out, a step ahead of "civilization." These boys talked about Savannah, back when it was nothing more than a stockade port town, the same as almost any Southerner talks about the inhumanity of living in New York City today. So they and their ancestors had gone up into the hills of Appalachia, and when somebody followed them they moved over to the next hill. They did, indeed, make their own whiskey and talk like they pleased and fire off their revolvers as the fancy took them. They had no means except a strong pair

[2]Excerpted from *The Nashville Sound: Bright Lights and Country Music* by Paul Hemphill. Simon & Schuster. '70. Copyright © 1970 by Paul Hemphill. Reprinted by permission of SIMON & SCHUSTER, Inc.

of hands and a good rifle and a broad back and an overworked mule, and a woman who could cook and have babies, and a God who maybe had a way out of all this if they would pay him homage now and then. These were the boys who carved planting land off the sides of jagged hills. These were the boys who trusted no one. These were the boys who sincerely thought it was a man's right, and also a good way to save money, to make his own whiskey. These were the boys who would later manage to justify slavery on the grounds that without these two-legged animals it would mean the crops would rot in the ground. These were the boys who had chosen the toughest life the country knew, who *wanted* to be alone and on the land and with their own kind of God, who knew how mean life could be but preferred it to the alternative of being around a lot of other people. These were the hillbillies, the people who held onto the old ways longer than anybody else in the country because that was *their* way. These were the poor, white, uneducated, conservative, hard-shell religious, Anglo-Saxon, Southern Appalachian, "free and untrammelled," whiskey-drinking, gun-toting, hookwormed, baby-making, rabbit-hunting Hill-Billies. Over the years, of course, the strain improved. Started voting. For Wallace.

And the old things they clung to included the music their ancestors had brought over from the British Isles. The music was simple and narrative, and it did what music is supposed to do: it took the mind off the miserable and lonely life these people had chosen, much the same as their religion did, and while they were making the music they were, in a sense, in another world. Once they had settled into the Appalachians, they began adapting the old songs with new words about the events going on around them, fitting the songs to their new surroundings: loneliness, poverty, religious faith, hard work, family life, bitter weather and Mother. There were few instruments, and those were always homemade. The dulcimer and the fiddle, the latter brought into the South by the first settlers, were the most popular in the beginning, and were later followed by the banjo (a Negro invention, popularized in the late nineteenth century), the guitar (late nineteenth century) and the mandolin (around 1900). The music was made for singing, in the distinctive, high-pitched, wailing, untrained Appalachian style, and until the commercial period began in the 1920's it was a highly personal music intended to be played and sung at home or on the village square or at such functions as barn-raisings and picnics and church meetings. This type of music can still be heard on the Grand Ole Opry, in fact, when Bill Monroe and the Bluegrass Boys fly into any of their old songs featuring banjo, mandolin and guitar with the high, nasal harmony that was taught a century ago by singing-school masters who traveled from one valley to another and taught shape-note singing through the church ("shape-note" because the shape of the note, rather than its position on a written scale, indicated its pitch). The church had other influences on what later became country music: songs meant more to the illiterate Southerners than sermons did, camp meetings offered a stage for the music, and the emotionalism of the Southern religion spilled over to the music.

All along, there were other influences working to change the music as the people began moving out of the hills and the tidewaters and the foothills of the South. The Negro, with a music all his own, wrought subtle changes; he taught them how to pick the guitar rather than merely strum it, and even today there is a term, "nigger-pickin'," denoting the use of the guitar as something much more than an accompanying instrument. The Negro also taught them what is today called "country blues" and has been commercially successful through Negro performers such as Blind Lemon Jefferson and many folk-pop stars of the Sixties. And still other changes were wrought by early industrialization, migration to the cities, exposure to the traveling medicine shows with their Swiss yodelers and black comedians and Hawaiian bands, and the tent shows with their dancing girls and Irish tenors. Once the country boy went back home—from the city, from a medicine show, from a railroad trip, from a jail, from wherever—he took with him new song ideas and new methods for singing or playing them: the yodel, "nigger-pickin'," railroad songs, the blues, the evils of the city, a new appreciation of the old homestead, the influences of jazz musicians he had heard on Beale Street in Memphis. Still, as commercialization lay right around the corner in the Twenties, country music remained distinctive. It was still "country," an honest expression of a distinctive breed, split into two branches: the sad, lonesome, bluesy stuff that had the psychological effect of a good cry; and the spirited, raise-hell-today-for-tomorrow-you-may-die stuff that had come over directly from Scotland and was meant to help a man forget his troubles. When the Twenties came, country music was still holed up in the Southern Appalachians and the Alabama farmlands and the Mississippi

Delta and the scrub-pine woods of East Texas. There was no such
thing as radio. The phonograph industry and even the sociolo-
gists were paying no attention to Southern music, deeming it too
crude for serious attention. Now and then a British folklorist
would come over and go back into the hills to make note of how
many of the old British ballads were still going strong in America.
Some American folklorists were beginning to notice, and write
about, this unique music of the Southern white, but getting others interested in it was like spitting into the wind. . . .

WSM, Inc., today announced that it has authorized a study to determine
the economic feasibility of building a new Grand Ole Opry House and
creating a major tourist attraction around it. The new complex would be
called "Opryland, U.S.A."
                                    —Press Release, October, 1968

In the spring of 1969, Columbia Records released an album
recorded in Nashville by Bob Dylan, a boy from Minnesota who
had become the darling of the folk-music crowd in New York.
Dylan's reputation had been built on protest songs like "Blowin'
in the Wind" and narrative ballads like "John Wesley Harding,"
sung in a mystical, plaintive, simple and direct way, and he had
become something of a legend to the young kids who were out
on the front lines raising money for Biafra and working on poverty programs in Mississippi and picketing grocery stores that sold
California grapes. But this newest Dylan album, "Nashville
Skyline," was something else. It had been recorded in Columbia's
Studio A on Music Row in Nashville, the same place where Marty
Robbins and Carl Smith and Johnny Cash regularly turned out
their country records. Indeed, the first song on the album was a
duet with Cash ("Girl from the North Country") and the album
liner was written by Cash, himself an idol of the nation's student
rebels but at heart a farm-hardened Arkansan who believes we
"ought to support our government's foreign policy" in Vietnam
and really doesn't cotton much to "hippahs." The album represented a new Bob Dylan, singing country songs with plain country
lyrics and the Nashville Sound in the background, and the advance orders were so strong that Columbia applied for a Gold Record certification (it would be Dylan's sixth) even before it had
hit the record shops.

Nashville was buzzing, of course, merely at the news that Dylan was coming to The Row to record ("He knows where the side-

men are at"). Interest quickened when the rumor of a Dylan-Cash duet leaked ("They say they just ran into each other in the parking lot and decided to sing something together"). And when the album was released, it was as though Nashville had been recognized by the UN ("Even the *title* is Nashville, man"). But nobody, *nobody but nobody*, was prepared for the ensuing interview with Dylan by *Newsweek*.

Dylan, the news magazine said, "seems to be rejecting the musical direction his many admirers have chosen for him in the past or would choose for him in the future." He was planning to appear on Cash's network television show during the summer, and he felt more at home in Nashville doing country music (if that is what it was) than he had ever felt in New York. "These are the type of songs that I always felt like writing when I've been alone to do so," he said. "Those [other] songs were all written in the New York atmosphere. I'd never have written any of them—or sung them the way I did—if I hadn't been sitting around listening to performers in New York cafés and the talk in all the dingy parlors. When I got to New York it was obvious that something was going on—folk music—and I did my best to learn and play it. I was just there at the right time with pen in hand. . . . I admire the spirit of the [new] music. It's got a good spirit. . . . I feel like writing a whole lot more of them, too." Later, Cash was to say about his friendship with Dylan: "Some writers have tried to make something out of it. They say they can't understand how we could be friends. Some people I like, some people I don't like. He can sing, and he *feels* what he sings. That's all there is to it. I regard him as a friend of mine because of that."

To some extent this summit meeting of the kings of country and folk music represented the future of "country music." That goes in quotations because as another decade approached it was becoming difficult to define what was "country" and what was not. Oh, sure, there was still pure, raw-gut country music: George Jones's East Texas twang ("I'll get over you/When the grass grows over me"), Wanda Jackson's bitchy God-Didn't-Make-Honky-Tonk-Angels preaching ("If you want some barroom swinger, I'm not the one/'Cause I don't think a girl's gotta drink to have fun"), or just about anything by Ernest Tubb, Roy Acuff, Porter Wagoner or Kitty Wells. But the Glen Campbells and the Bobby Russells and the Eddy Arnolds and the Roger Millers were crossing over into pop music ("pop-country," they called it in

Nashville) so often that what was left of pure country music was in a small corner of the music world by itself: on rural radio stations, at barn dances, at annual fiddlers' contests in the Southern mountains, at the Grand Ole Opry. For kicks, take a look at the Top Ten records on *Billboard*'s Hot Country Singles chart for the week ending January 11, 1969: five of them had transcended the country-music field for one reason or another: Cash's "Daddy Sang Bass" because it was Cash, Campbell's "Wichita Lineman" because it was pop, Waylon Jennings' "Yours Love" because it was smooth, Tom T. Hall's "Ballad of Forty Dollars" because it was folkish, and Eddy Arnold's "They Don't Make Love Like They Used To" because it was Arnold. Any of those recordings could have merited play—or were being played—on "pop" radio stations. And even the pure hard-country music was being discovered, often because it was considered "quaint," by college students: Bill Monroe and the Bluegrass Boys, Flatt & Scruggs (who split in '69), Acuff, Wagoner and George Jones. Was there going to be a fusing of the music, meaning there would no longer be a difference between country, pop, folk, blues, jazz, all of the rest? Would Roy Acuff, at his age, after a lifetime of singing the stuff he knew best, would even Roy Acuff begin to shift toward the middle? "You go down into these little country towns and you'll find they still like the Acuffs," said Jack Stapp of Tree Publishing in Nashville, perhaps summing up the future as well as anyone could. "There'll always be country, and then there'll always be pop music. But the interlocking will be so that a certain number of country songs will go pop every year. I don't think it'll ever become completely *one* music." And so what the Dylan album meant, in the end, was that folk music had come country music's way and country music had gone out to meet it. Temporarily. Bob Dylan is no more ready to pack his rucksack and hitchhike to a new life in Nashville than Johnny Cash is planning to take June and the kids to New York and get a job singing in a cabaret in the East Village. But Dylan does some things Cash likes, and Cash has been some places Dylan wishes he had been, and they are both big enough to borrow from each other. It makes for better folk music and for better country music. When the barriers fall and communication is established, it helps everybody. God. Liberalism at its peak.

ELVIS, OR THE IRONIES OF A SOUTHERN
IDENTITY[3]

Elvis was the most popular entertainer in the world, but no-where as popular as in his native South. In the last years of his ca-reer, his audience in other parts of the country was generally centered in the original "fifties" fans whose youth and music were defined by Elvis, and in the lower or working class people who saw in Elvis some glamorized image of their own values. In the South, however, the pattern of Elvis' popularity tended to cut across age barriers and class lines which were themselves a less recognizable thing in a region in which almost no one is more than a genera-tion or two away from poverty, and where "class" in small commu-nities might have more to do with family and past status than with money. Among Southern youth, Elvis was not a relic from a musi-cal past; he was still one of the vital forces behind a Southern rock, which though different now from his, still echoes the rhythms which his music had fused out of the region. His numer-ous concerts in the South could not exhaust the potential audi-ence. At his death, leading politicians and ministers from the South joined the people on the street in eulogizing him. Local ra-dio and television stations ran their own specials in addition to the syndicated or national programs. Halftime ceremonies at the Lib-erty Bowl were in tribute to him. When someone commented on national TV that the Presleys were "white trash," it was a regional slur, not just a personal one. The white South expressed love, grief, and praise for Elvis from all age groups at virtually every level of the social, intellectual, and economic structures.

The phenomenon of such widespread sectional regard and emotional intensity went beyond the South's usual pride in the success of "one of our own." The emotion became more puzzling if one listened to some of the reasons offered to explain it: Elvis loved his mother; Elvis' heart was broken; Elvis loved Jesus; Elvis was the American Dream. Such reasons for loving and mourning Elvis seemed strange because, on the surface at least, they were so tangential to Elvis himself or to the musical or cultural impact he unquestionably did have. How, in the face of his vitality and

[3]Reprint of an essay by Linda Ray Pratt, professor of English at the University of Nebraska-Lincoln. Copyright © 1979 by Linda Ray Pratt. Used by permission of the author.

defiance of convention, could one love Elvis because he loved Jesus? And how, in a man expressing nothing if not undisguised sexuality, could one love Elvis because he was so good to his mother? But people, especially those beyond the age group of his original teen fans, often did say such things. Merle Haggard's "From Graceland to the Promised Land," with its emphasis on Elvis' mother's death and his faith in Jesus, is, after all, the perfect Southern folk song about Elvis. The South's involvement with Elvis is sincere, but most of the expressed reasons for it do not reach very far, and some of them seem patently false. They are the myths sent up to justify the emotion and to obscure its source. The emotions spring from associations with a reality the South collectively prefers to conceal and yet constantly experiences. The paradox of Elvis was that he was able simultaneously to reveal the reality of the modern South while concealing it in a myth of the American Dream. He was at once both "King" and outsider.

The myth of Elvis which the South voices is in part very familiar. He is the sharecropper's son who made millions, the Horatio Alger story in drawl. Almost everyone who knew him assured us that, despite the money and fame, "he never changed" (no one remarks how tragic such a static condition would be, were it possible). He never got over his mother's death (in 1958); he was humble and polite; he doted on his little girl; he loved his home town; he never forgot where he came from. He had wealth, yes; but in the tradition of those who love Jesus, he was uncomfortable with riches when others were poor and so gave millions of dollars away to the less fortunate. The American success story turned to altruism. Even his money was not tainted, just dollars freely given in exchange for entertainment so good it always seemed a bargain. Unlike some others whose success was a ticket out of the South and into the broader, happier American identity, Elvis remained in Memphis. His regional loyalty when he could have lived anywhere deeply complimented the South. Graceland was a new image of the Southern plantation, this time free from associations with slavery and a guilt-ridden past. The very gates had musical notes on them. He was a good boy and a good ole boy. Elvis himself seemed to believe this vision; certainly he played to it in his "family" movies, his sacred music, and in his "American Trilogy" dominated by "Dixie." It was a sentimental myth, but, then, W. J. Cash has called Southerners "the most sentimental people in history" (*The Mind of the South*, p. 130).

Elvis' fame initially grew out of an image in opposition to the one the myth attempts to disguise. He was scandalous, sexual, defiant of all authority. He was preached against from the pulpit as an immoral force. In a blackboard jungle, he was the juvenile delinquent. On the streets, he was a hood. Socially, he was a "greaser." Economically, he was "poor white," a gentler rendition of "white trash." Maybe he loved Jesus, but even his Christmas songs could be dirty. In songs like "Santa Claus Is Back In Town" he played with the conventions of Christmas music in order to startle and subvert.

This image of Elvis, the rocker with "a dirty, dirty feeling," "born standing up and talking back," never fully disappeared. His last few movies, like a lot of the lyrics he improvised in concert, were sprinkled with off-color jokes and plays on words. His 1976 image was as excessive and extravagant as his 1956 image, though not in the same ways. The violence still flowed out of the karate movements, the sexuality in such songs as "Burning Love." In concert, his emotional passion sometimes transfigured such schmaltzy songs of lost love and broken hearts as "Hurt" or "You Gave Me a Mountain" into rich autobiographical moments. Even the obscene subversion of Christmas showed up again in "Merry Christmas, Baby."

The Elvis of the sentimental myth would never have changed musical or cultural history, but the authentic Elvis who did so was transformed into a legend obscuring what the man, the music, or the image really meant. Although some elements of the myth were commonly associated with Elvis throughout the country, in the South—particularly the white South—the myth was insisted upon and pushed to its extremes. The question is why. Jimmy Carter loves his mother and Jesus, too, but the South has not rewarded him with uncritical devotion. The real Elvis, both early and late, might have been severely criticized, but even his drug-involved death is called a "heart attack," the ten drugs the autopsy found in his body merely the "prescription medicines" of a sick and heartbroken man who kept pushing himself because he did not want to disappoint the fans. Those who have argued that people projected onto Elvis anything they liked because his image was essentially vacuous are mistaken; if anything, the image is too rich in suggestion to be acknowledged fully or directly.

Some critics attribute the sentimental myth of Elvis to the cleverness of Colonel Parker and the cooperation of Elvis himself. To do so is to oversimplify a complex phenomenon and to misread a generation's genuine mythmaking as merely another shrewd "sell" campaign. For anyone less significant than Elvis, the path that Colonel Parker apparently advised by way of numbingly stupid movies and empty music would have been the path to sure oblivion. The 1968 Black Leather television special saved Elvis from that, but allegedly against the advice of Parker who wanted the show to be all Christmas music. Elvis, pursued by the myth and under pressure to confirm it, kept to himself and never told the public anything. The Colonel was smart enough to promote the myth, but it was the authentic handiwork of a society that needed a legend to justify the identification it felt with such a figure. After Elvis died, the Brentwood, Tennessee, Historical Society even supplied the Presley genealogy. The family was, of course, completely respectable, producing "renowned professors, doctors, judges, ministers" in every generation until poverty overcame them during Reconstruction.

C. Vann Woodward has said that the South's experience is atypical of the American experience, that where the rest of America has known innocence, success, affluence, and an abstract and disconnected sense of place, the South has known guilt, poverty, failure, and a concrete sense of roots and place ("The Search for Southern Identity" in *The Burden of South History*). These myths collide in Elvis. His American success story was always acted out within its Southern limitations. No matter how successful Elvis became in terms of fame and money, he remained fundamentally disreputable in the minds of many Americans. Elvis had rooms full of gold records earned by million-copy sales, but his best rock and roll records were not formally honored by the people who control, if not the public taste, the rewarding of the public taste. Perhaps this is always the fate of innovators; awards are created long after the form is created. His movies made millions but could not be defended on artistic grounds. *The New York Times* view of his fans was "the men favoring leisure suits and sideburns, the women beehive hairdos, purple eyelids and tight stretch pants" (*New York Times* story by Wayne King, 8 Jan. 1978). Molly Ivins, trying to explain in *The New York Times* the crush of people and "genuine emotion" in Memphis when Elvis died would conclude, "It is not required that love be in impeccable taste." Later, in the year after his death, Mike Royko would sarcastically suggest that Elvis' body and effects be sent to Egypt in exchange for the King Tut exhibit. ("So in terms of sheer popularity, no other American dead body can stand up to Presley's.") The "Doonesbury" cartoon strip would see fit to run a two-weeks sequence in which "Boopsie" would go visit Elvis' grave. Her boyfriend puts her down with, "2,000,000 necrophiliacs can't be wrong." Elvis' sheer commercial value commanded respect, but no amount of success could dispel the aura of strangeness about him. He remained an outsider in the American culture that adopted his music, his long hair, his unconventional clothes, and his freedom of sexual movement.

Although he was the world's most popular entertainer, to like Elvis a lot was suspect, a lapse of taste. It put one in beehives and leisure suits, in company with "necrophiliacs" and other weird sorts. The inability of Elvis to transcend his lack of reputability despite a history-making success story confirms the Southern sense that the world outside thinks Southerners are freaks, illiterates, Snopeses, sexual perverts, lynchers. I cannot call this sense a Southern "paranoia" because ten years outside the South has all too often confirmed the frequency with which non-Southerners express such views. Not even the presidency would free LBJ and Jimmy Carter from such ridicule. At the very moment in which Southerners proclaim most vehemently the specialness of Elvis, the greatness of his success, they understand it to mean that no Southern success story can ever be sufficient to satisfy a suspicious America.

And Elvis was truly different, in all those tacky Southern ways one is supposed to rise above with money and sophistication. He was a pork chops and brown gravy man. He liked peanut butter and banana sandwiches. He had too many cars, and they were too pink. He liked guns, and capes, and a Venus de Milo water fountain in the entry at Graceland. I once heard about 1958 that he had painted the ceiling at Graceland dark blue with little silver stars that twinkled in the dark. His taste never improved, and he never recanted anything. He was the sharecropper's son in the big house, and it always showed.

Compounding his case was the fact that Elvis didn't always appear fully white. Not sounding white was his first problem, and white radio stations were initially reluctant to play his records. Not to be clearly white was dangerous because it undermined the black-white rigidities of a segregated society, and to blur those definitions was to reveal the falseness at the core of segregation.

Racial ambiguity is both the internal moral condemnation and the social destruction of a racist society which can only pretend to justify itself by abiding by its own taboos. Yet all Southerners know, despite the sternest Jim Crow laws, that more than two hundred years of racial mixing has left many a Southerner racially ambiguous. White Southerners admit only the reality of blacks who have some white blood, but, of course, the knife cuts both ways. Joe Christmas and Charles Bon. Desiree's Baby. In most pictures, Elvis might resemble a blue-eyed Adonis, but in some of those early black and white photographs, his eyes sultry, nostrils flared, lips sullen, he looked just that—black and white. And he dressed like blacks. His early wardrobe came from Lansky Brothers in Memphis. Maybe truck drivers wore greasy hair and long sideburns, but only the blacks were wearing zoot suits and pegged pants with pink darts in them. Country singers might sequin cactus and saddles on satin shirts, Marty Robbins would put a pink carnation on a white sport coat, and Johnny Cash would be the man in black. Only Elvis would wear a pink sport coat with a black velvet collar. "The Memphis Flash," he was sometimes called.

The music was the obvious racial ambiguity. Elvis' use of black styles and black music angered many Southern blacks who resented the success he won with music that black artists had originated but could not sell beyond the "race record" market of a segregated commercial world. In interviews today, these black blues musicians usually say that Elvis stole everything from them, an understandable complaint but one that nevertheless ignores his fusion of black music with white country to create a genuinely new sound. He was the Hillbilly Cat singing "Blue Moon of Kentucky" and "That's All Right (Mama)." Elvis' role in fusing the native music of poor Southern whites and poor Southern blacks into rock and roll is the best known aspect of his career and his greatest accomplishment.

Students of rock always stress this early music, but the sentimental myth gives it less attention, though the records always sold better in the South than in any other region. The music in the myth is more often the love ballads and the Protestant hymns. Yet the music that was in reality most important to Southerners was the music most closely tied to Southern origins. Elvis himself seemed to understand this; compare, for example, his 1974 concert album from Memphis's Mid-South Coliseum (the "Graceland" album) with any other concert album. The music I remember hearing most was music like "Mystery Train," "One Night," "Lawdy Miss Clawdy," "Heartbreak Hotel," "Peace in the Valley," "Blue Christmas," and "American Trilogy." For Southerners, this fusion of "Dixie," "All My Trials," and "The Battle Hymn of the Republic" has nothing to do with the rest of America, although its popularity around the country suggests that other Americans do relate it to their own history. The trilogy seems to capture Southern history through the changes of the civil rights movement and the awareness of black suffering which had hitherto largely been excluded from popular white images of Southern history. The piece could not have emerged before the seventies because only then had the "marching" brough a glimmer of hope. Even Elvis could not have sung this trilogy in New York's Madison Square Garden before there was some reason for pride and hope in the South. Elvis was right to make the song his; it is an appropriate musical history from one whose music moved always in the fused racial experiences of the region's oppressed. Rock and roll, taking inside it rhythm and blues and country, was the rhythm of Southern life, Southern problems, and Southern hopes. It is not coincidence that rock and roll emerged almost simultaneously with the civil rights movement, that both challenged the existing authority, and that both were forces for "integration."

The most stunning quality about Elvis and the music was the sexuality, yet the sentimental myth veers away from this disturbing complexity into the harmlessly romantic. Elvis might be "nice looking" or "cute" or perhaps "sexy," but not sexual. The sexuality he projected was complicated because it combined characteristics and appeals traditionally associated with both males and females. On one hand, he projected masculine aggression and an image of abandoned pleasure, illicit thrills, back alley liaisons and, on the other hand, a quality of tenderness, vulnerability, and romantic emotion. Andy Warhol captured something of this diversified sexuality in his portrait of Elvis, caught in a threatening stance with a gun in his hand but with the face softened in tone and line. The image made Elvis the perfect lover by combining the most appealing of male and female characteristics and satisfying both the physical desire for sensual excitement and the emotional need for loving tenderness. The music echoed the physical pleasure in rhythm and the emotional need in lyrics that said "Love Me," "Love Me Tender," "Don't," "I Want You I Need You

I Love You," and "Don't Be Cruel." Unlike many later rock stars whose music would voice an assault on women, Elvis' music usually portrayed an emotional vulnerability to what women could do *to* him, as well as what he could do *for* them. When the public's notion of his heartbroken private life confirmed this sense of vulnerability, the image took on renewed power. Despite the evidence in the music or the long hair and lashes and full, rounded features, most Elvis fans would deny that his appeal is vaguely androgynous. Many male and female fans talk about Elvis as an ideal male image but would probably find it threatening to traditions of sexual identity to admit that the ideal male figure might indeed combine traditional male characteristics with some which are freely admitted only in women. In the South where sex roles are bound up with the remnants of a chivalric "way of life," open sexuality was allowable only in the "mysterious" lives of blacks, and permissible sexual traits in whites were rigidly categorized by sex. But the image of Elvis goes behind these stereotypes to some ideal of sexuality that combines the most attractive elements in each of them.

Women's sexual imaginations of Elvis have rarely been openly expressed, in part because women weren't supposed to have any explicit sexual fantasies and in part because those who did were perhaps least likely, because of the cultural and regional prohibitions, to admit them. Despite the mass of published material about Elvis, almost nothing of a serious nature by women has been printed. One remarkable exception is a short story by Julie Hecht, "I Want You I Need You I Love You" in *Harper's* (May 1978). Hecht's story makes the only serious effort I have seen to reveal those characteristics which gave Elvis' sexual appeal such complexity and power. The woman in the story remembers first imagining his kiss when she was twelve and didn't know what came after the kiss. Twenty years later in her fantasy of August 1977, she is able to "save" Elvis' life by getting him on a good health food diet. They become "best of friends," and she has her moment of tenderness: "I did get to touch him. I touched his hands, I touched his face, we hugged, we kissed, I kissed his hands, I kissed his face, I touched his face, I touched his arms, I touched his eyes, I touched his hair, I saw his smile, I heard his voice, I saw him move, I heard him laugh, I heard him sing" (*Harper's,* p. 67). This passage illustrates the obsessive physical attraction that combined with the illusion that Elvis was really sweet, tender, and in need of loving care. Seeing or hearing Elvis was never enough; one had to try to touch him. In life, such fans tore at his clothes and his person; in death, they visit his grave. Does any woman really care whether or not Elvis loves his mother or Jesus? But I never met a female fan who did not detest Priscilla. "Somebody ought to put a bullet through her," a pleasant faced middle-aged saleswoman in a bookstore once told me.

Elvis said he grew sideburns because he wanted to look like truck drivers, and many such men would later want to look like him. One important element in Elvis' sexual appeal for men seemed to be the acting out of the role of the "hood" who got the girl, won the fight, and rose above all the economic powerlessness of real hoods. Men who because of class and economic binds knew their own limitations seemed especially attracted to this aspect of the image. They wore their hair like his, affected his mannerisms, sang with his records. Men too sophisticated to betray themselves in such overt ways betrayed themselves in other ways. I remember a highly educated man rhapsodizing about how phallic the black leather suit was that Elvis wore in his 1968 television appearance. When Elvis aged and put on weight, men were his cruelest detractors. They seemed to take his appearance as a personal offense.

Beyond the money, the power, the fame, there was always at some level this aspect of Elvis, the American Dream in its Southern variation. Like other great Southern artists, Elvis revealed those characteristics of our culture which we know better than outsiders to be part of the truth. In Elvis was also the South that is bizarre, or violent, or darkly mysterious, the South called the grotesque in Faulkner or O'Connor. Perhaps this is why a book like *Elvis: What Happened?* could not damage the appeal. The hidden terrors, pain, and excesses of the private life which the book reveals, despite its mean-spirited distortions, only make the image more compelling in its familiarity. Even his drug problem had a familiar Southern accent—precription medicines, cough syrups, diet pills.

Elvis' South is not the old cotton South of poor but genteel aristocrats. His Mississippi is not that of Natchez. Elvis is the Mississippi of pulpwood, sharecroppers, small merchants. His Memphis had nothing to do with riverboats or the fabled Beale Street. Elvis' Memphis was the post–World War II city of urban sprawl, racial antagonism, industrial blight, slums, Humes High. He

walked the real Beale Street. Despite Graceland, and "Dixie" in
Madison Square Garden, Elvis was the antithesis of the Rhett and
Scarlett South. But no one living in the South today ever knew
the Rhett and Scarlett South. Southerners themselves go to
Natchez as to a tourist attraction. Elvis' South was the one that
most Southerners really experience, the South where not even
the interstate can conceal the poverty, where industrial affluence
threatens the land and air which have been so much a part of our
lives, where racial violence touches deep inside the home, where
even our successes cannot overcome the long reputation of our
failures. Even Graceland is not really beautiful. Squeezed in on
all sides by the sprawl of gas stations, banks, shopping plazas, and
funeral homes, Elvis' beloved home is an image of the South that
has been "new" now for over fifty years.

Elvis evoked the South of modern reality with a fidelity he
could not himself escape. The South rewarded him with its most
cherished myths, but Elvis' tragedy was that he got caught in the
contradictions. We only wanted to be able to claim that he was
a good boy who loved Jesus. He apparently needed to become
that, to live out the mythic expectations. He hungered for approval. The problem was that most of what Elvis really was could
never be so transmogrified. He *was* the king of rock and roll, but
he was uncomfortable with what the title implied. Linda Thompson has said that in his later years he hated hard rock. The further
he moved from the conventions of the romantic myth, the more
he proclaimed them. The more drugs he used, the more he sup-
ported law and order. When the counter culture he helped to
usher in became widespread, he thought of helping the FBI as an
undercover agent. How could he not be schizophrenic at the end,
balancing the rock myth he created, the sentimental myth he
adopted, and the emotional needs that made him like anyone
else? He was destroyed by having to be what he was and wanting
to be what he thought he ought to be. The Jesus-loving boy singing dirty Christmas songs. "One Night" and "How Great Thou
Art."

After Elvis died, it was necessary to deify him. It isn't after all,
very becoming to grieve for a rock idol who died, as *The New York
Times* once put it, "puffy and drug-wasted." But saying what and
why one grieved was difficult. The South has had a lot of practice
mythologizing painful and ambiguous experiences into glamorous and noble abstractions. So it was from Graceland to the

Promised Land. Rex Humbard told us that Elvis found peace in
Jesus, and Billy Graham assured us that Elvis was in Heaven. Billy
was even looking forward to visiting him there. A disc jockey
playing "How Great Thou Art" reflects at the end of the record,
"And he certainly was." In Tupelo the Elvis Presley Memorial
Foundation is building a $125,000 Chapel of Inspiration in his
memory. Memphis will put a 50-ton bronze statue on a river
bluff. Priscilla wants their daughter to remember, most of all, his
humbleness. He loved his Jesus, his daughter, his lost wife. He
loved his daddy. He loved the South. He was a great humanitari-
an. "God saw that he needed some rest and called him home to
be with Him," the tombstone reads. Maybe all of this is even true.
The apotheosis of Elvis demands such perfection because his
death confirmed the tragic frailty, the violence, the intellectual
poverty, the extravagance of emotion, the loneliness, the suffering, the sense of loss. Almost everything about his death, including the enterprising cousin who sold the casket pictures to
National Enquirer, dismays, but nothing can detract from Elvis
himself. Even this way, he is as familiar as next door, last year, the
town before.

Greil Marcus wrote in his book *Mystery Train: Images of America in Rock 'n' Roll Music* that Elvis created a beautiful illusion, a
fantasy that shut nothing out. The opposite was true. The fascina-
tion was the reality always showing through the illusion—the illusion of wealth and the psyche of poverty; the illusion of success
and the pinch of ridicule; the illusion of invincibility and the tragedy of frailty; the illusion of complete control and the reality of
inner chaos. In Faulkner's *Absalom, Absalom!* Shreve thinks that
Quentin hates the South. He does not understand that Quentin
is too caught in it ever to have thought of such a question, just
as Elvis was and just as we were in Elvis. Elvis had all the freedom
the world can offer and could escape nothing. What chance that
the South could escape him, reflecting it as he did?

Southerners do not love the old Confederacy because it was
a noble ideal, but because the suffering of the past occasioned by
it has formed our hearts and souls, both good and evil. But we celebrate the past with cheap flags, cliche slogans, decorative license
plates, decaled ash trays, and a glorious myth of a Southern "way
of life" no one today ever lived. And Southerners do not love Elvis because he loved Jesus or anyone else. The Elvis trinkets, his
picture on waste cans or paperweights or T-shirts or glowing in

the dark from a special frame, all pay the same kind of homage as the trinkets in worship of the past. People outside the Elvis phenomenon may think such commercialization demeans the idol and the idolater. But for those who have habitually disguised the reality of their culture from even themselves, it is hard to show candidly what and why one loves. In impeccable taste. By the most sentimental people in history.

THE MUSIC THAT CHANGED THE WORLD[4]

Pop music in the pre-rock Fifties was prized for its innocuousness. Placid citizens sang along with Mitch Miller, numbly hummed the hits of Perry Como and Vaughn Monroe and beamed vacantly as Patti Page posed the musical question "How much is that doggie in the window?" You had to be a kid in those years to appreciate how oppressively lame it all seemed, how deeply dull. And then, suddenly, there was rock & roll, and the world felt remade. Rock provided a salutary tongue in the ear to the overstuffed status quo, and eventually displaced it. Long-overdue thanks for delivering this heaven-sent revolution now go to the first Rock and Roll Hall of Fame inductees, a group of artists as unlikely in their impact as they are irreplaceable in their accomplishments.

None of the pioneers commended here was a product of privilege or power or extended education; they were outsiders, essentially provincial. Yet together they changed the world in ways that still reverberate, thirty years later.

Consider Elvis Presley. Unlike his fellow honorees, Presley was neither a songwriter nor an instrumental virtuoso. But his youthful, sultry pout has defined the look of teen idols from Conway Twitty to Simon Le Bon; and his epochal artistic stance—that of the proud young bopcat blasting out a niche for his new sound in the American musical tradition—has been assumed by every upstart rocker with a new twist on the old Big Beat. Presley's imposing position in rock would be inarguable solely on the

[4]Reprint of a magazine article by senior editor Kurt Loder. From *Rolling Stone*. p49–50. F. 13, '86. By Straight Arrow Publishers, Inc. © 1986. All rights reserved. Reprinted by permission.

basis of the five classic singles he slammed out for Sun Records in 1954 and 1955: "That's All Right," "Good Rockin' Tonight," "Milk Cow Blues Boogie," "Baby, Let's Play House" and "Mystery Train." (Each disc is also adorned with the sound of Scotty Moore inventing the rockabilly guitar style.) In successfully declaring himself a poor white Southerner aflame with the spirit of black Southern blues (and a-twitch with that music's forbidden carnality), he was a cultural A-bomb. That he was still capable, as late as 1972—after all the years of wealth and indulgence—of cutting a track as ferociously potent as "Burning Love" was a testament to the vastness of his creative reserves.

The career of James Brown, whose impact on the structure of modern rock has surpassed even that of Presley, is ripe for revised assessment. His stylistic innovations are of a number sufficient to have distinguished several less protean careers. The gospel- and doo-wop-drenched records he cut for the Federal and King labels through the early Sixties—"I'll Go Crazy," "Think," "This Old Heart"—are flat-out rock & roll as impassioned as anything in the canon. His heartbroken, scraped-raw vocal style prefigured the soul music that evolved in the later Sixties. And his formidable powers as a stage performer—devastatingly preserved on 1963's *Live at the Apollo*—set standards for pacing, endurance and ensemble cohesion that have yet to be bettered. (When you see Springsteen go into his can't-stop-now shtick toward the end of one of his marathon shows—the robe over the sweat-soaked shoulders, the reluctant exit, the last-minute sprint back to the mike to start all over again—you're watching a tribute from the Boss to the Master.) In 1964, with "Out of Sight," Brown began reassembling traditional R&B rhythms into a whole new "thang" (as he put it) and set the course that black popular music (and the white dance pop that has so often followed its lead) would take for the next twenty years, via such heirs-to-the-funk as Sly Stone, George Clinton and Prince. He also supplied anthems for the rising tide of black consciousness ("Say It Loud—I'm Black and I'm Proud"), turned his streetwise eye to social issues ("King Heroin," "Don't Be a Drop-Out") and, along the way, with such sides as "Brother Rapp (Part I)," laid the base for the rap-music movement of the Eighties. When James Brown dubbed himself Soul Brother Number One, nobody argued. He's still performing today—and still proving it.

Even more effectively than Brown, Ray Charles introduced black-gospel elements into rock with a series of records for Atlantic that are still awesome aural artifacts: "I've Got A Woman," "Hallelujah I Love Her So," the astonishing "What'd I Say" and the landmark concert LPs *Ray Charles at Newport* and *In Person*. These records showed Charles to be an extraordinary pianist, bandleader and—with a voice that could swing effortlessly from a gravelly growl to a piercing falsetto—possibly the greatest blues singer of his generation. He was certainly the most influential; there would be no Joe Cocker, to name one contemporary acolyte, without him. Charles was instrumental in demolishing the boundaries that segregated American music, topping the pop charts in 1962 with a double-sided single that paired exquisitely soulful renditions of two country classics: Don Gibson's "I Can't Stop Loving You" and Ted Daffan's "Born to Lose." He went on to score several more country-inspired hits, demonstrating that a good song is a good song, no matter who wrote it. Over the years Charles has also brought his inimitable blues sensibility to bear on traditional pop ("Georgia on My Mind"), film themes ("In the Heat of the Night"), Beatles tunes ("Yesterday," "Eleanor Rigby"), even Coca-Cola commercials. Like all the great rockers, he has become more than just a rock & roller. Ray Charles stands today, thirty-five years after his first R&B hit, as a giant of American music.

Little Richard and Jerry Lee Lewis were giants of attitude, blowing the lid off the boxed-up social notions of the mid-Fifties. Unlike Presley—who at heart was a soft-spoken, well-mannered Southern boy—Richard and Lewis appeared not merely wild but totally out of control. Both played piano, but not in a way likely to gladden the heart of the average music teacher. Both flaunted long hair and alien attire: zoot suits, bop shirts, fake leopard and lamé. These men had an answer to all the naysayers of the stultifying adult world. . . .

Little Richard and Jerry Lee each claimed to be the King of Rock & Roll—a point it would be difficult (and, in Lewis' case, perhaps dangerous) to argue. Together, they defined the outer limits of rock abandon. "Tutti Frutti," Richard's 1955 debut hit, was the seminal stupid-fabulous rock record. Lyrically, it meant zip, and yet, once heard by thrill-starved ears, it seemed to mean everything: get loose, get crazy, get free. Here was the original exhortation to kick out the jams. Richard's voice was a monumental screaming machine, and the sax-packed jump bands with which he was paired provided maximum liftoff. Within the grooves of his great hits there beats still the heart of the mind-blown rock & roll moment. Richard's legacy is apparent in the work of Mitch Ryder, Otis Redding (an early idolater whose 1960 single "Shout Bamalama" is a direct *hommage*), the Beatles (who covered two of his tunes and appropriated his trademark "oooooh!") and every other glorious misfit who ever donned *outré* duds and mounted a stage. The original, however, has never been exceeded.

Richard's legendary antics may have been equaled, however, by Jerry Lee in his piano-battering prime. Like Little Richard, Lewis was an erstwhile Bible student who went on to put the fear of God into parents and other authority figures. Equipped with a honky-tonk piano style inherited from Moon Mullican and a high, distinctive voice that could make any song his own, Lewis exploded onto the scene like Elvis in an ominous mood. That Lewis' rock & roll reputation rests on just four Sun singles—"Whole Lotta Shakin' Goin' On" and "Great Balls of Fire," in 1957; "Breathless" and "High School Confidential," in 1958—is inadequate tribute to his talent. His market potential was never fully served by Sun's release strategies, and the intercontinental uproar that followed his December 1957 marriage to Myra Brown, his thirteen-year-old third cousin (and third wife), stopped his rock career cold. He fought his way back into the country market; but unlike other aging rockers who tone down their act for the C&W crowd, Lewis is still as likely to pound out rock & roll onstage as he is to cuddle up to anyone's more sedate expectations. His relentlessly stormy personal saga—the women, the booze, the pills—is a prototype of the lifestyle that's come to be known as Sex, Drugs and Rock & Roll. That he's still living is but one of the man's many amazing accomplishments.

If Lewis and Little Richard had tapped into something primal—and a little scary—Chuck Berry and Buddy Holly were more reassuring. In their work, the world of the American teenager—cars and girls and love, all still-innocent fun—found its most vivid depiction. Berry, a black hairdresser with a love of country music, wrote the book on rock guitar (Keith Richards, George Thorogood and countless hard rockers are still reading it), and he invented the duckwalk. These accomplishments alone would be enough to secure him a place in the hall of fame. But it is his songs that confirm Berry's primacy beyond cavil. Along with his exuberant salutes to cars ("Maybellene," "No Particular Place to Go"), girls ("Carol," "Nadine") and the eternal dilemmas of teendom ("School Day," "Almost Grown"), Berry was the first important rock songwriter to celebrate the music itself, in such timeless salutes as "Roll Over Beethoven," "Rock and Roll Music" and "Johnny B. Goode." His songs will be played in backwoods bars and big-time arenas as long as guitar bands roam the earth: a clarion call across the generations to keep the musical faith.

Buddy Holly was Berry's cultural opposite: a country boy with a taste for R&B. In the space of less than two years—from February 25th, 1957, when he recorded "That'll Be the Day" at Norman Petty's small studio in Clovis, New Mexico, to February 3rd, 1959, when he was killed in a plane crash near Clear Lake, Iowa—Holly created a phenomenal body of material, much of it not released until after his death. His hits—credited to his band, the Crickets, on the Brunswick label ("Maybe Baby," "Think It Over," "Oh, Boy!") and as solo efforts on Coral ("Peggy Sue," "Rave On," "It Doesn't Matter Anymore")—sound as fresh and unmannered and heartfelt today as they did three decades ago. Holly was the first major rock star to strap on a Stratocaster, and his band exemplified the now-classic rock & roll lineup: songwriting frontman accompanied by electric guitars, bass and drums. He was the first to experiment with strings and with studio effects, double-tracking his voice on "Words of Love" and employing the simple sound of knee-slapping hands for percussion on "Everyday." His songs have been covered by the Beatles, the Rolling Stones and countless others, and his influence can be strongly felt in the work of such disparate artists as Bob Dylan, John Fogerty, Ray Davies and Ric Ocasek of the Cars, to name but a few. And beyond the records released during Holly's lifetime lie songs of equal brilliance: "Crying, Waiting, Hoping," "Peggy Sue Got Married," "Learning the Game." More than a quarter century after his death, Buddy Holly is still missed.

Rock's great voices defined a now-vanished era—a time of true love and innocent pleasures, a place in the heart beyond irony and cynicism. None did this more memorably than Sam Cooke, Fats Domino and the Everly Brothers. Cooke, the Chicago-bred son of a Baptist minister, brought to rock & roll a voice of supernal sweetness and an effortless mastery of even the lightest lyrics: "You Send Me," "Only Sixteen," "Wonderful World,"

"Twistin' the Night Away," "Having a Party." He could bear down on bluesier material, too, as in the superlative "Bring It On Home to Me" (with Lou Rawls providing gospel-style response). Cooke's hits have been covered by everyone from Aretha Franklin and the Animals to Southside Johnny and Dr. Hook, and echoes of his unforgettable voice can be heard in the work of Rod Stewart, Al Green and Paul Simon, among others. The sad fact that Cooke's most stirring achievement was the posthumously released "A Change Is Gonna Come" suggests what further marvels would surely be ours had he lived.

Fats Domino, more than any other hall-of-fame honoree, brought to rock & roll the distinct sound of a city. The city was New Orleans, and its native rolling rhythms, apparent in most of the Fat Man's delightful hits, exerted a profound influence (via trans-Caribbean radio signals) on the development of Jamaica ska, the precursor of reggae. Domino was an unabashed apostle of fun and good feelings ("I'm in Love Again," "Blueberry Hill," "Whole Lotta Loving"), even at his most purportedly brokenhearted ("Ain't It a Shame," "I'm Walkin'," "Blue Monday"). His lusciously slurred delivery, set atop a classic Crescent City musical base thick with saxophones and clumps of block-chord piano, created an atmosphere of foot-tapping amiability. Fats seldom deviated from this patented style, but the style itself was endlessly appealing. Domino's influence has been deceptively subtle outside the New Orleans school of rock. The Beatles' "Lady Madonna" was an affectionate take on the man's *oeuvre* (and so expert that Fats covered it himself), and Rockin' Sidney's "My Toot Toot" seemed almost written to order for the version Domino recorded with Doug Kershaw last year. Were his still-in-print records to disappear from the racks tomorrow, his lovable, rollicking legacy would glow on in the hearts of all who'd ever heard them.

The Everly Brothers contributed a final, indispensable element to the glorious stylistic stew of rock & roll: teen sorrow. Twined together, the exhilarating voices of Don and Phil Everly conjured up the sound of one heart breaking—a pattern set with their first hit, "Bye Bye Love," and continued through "All I Have to Do Is Dream," "Cathy's Clown," "Walk Right Back" and their penultimate Top Ten entry, "Crying in the Rain." There were healing respites: "Wake Up Little Susie," "Devoted to You," "('Til) I Kissed You." But the Everlys' soaring harmonies, distilled from the country tradition in which they were raised, suggested a world of loss and loneliness that less sensitive spirits—grown-ups!—could never know with such heart-crushing intimacy. The Everlys were very fine songwriters when they turned their hands to it: Don penned "('Til) I Kissed You" and "So Sad (To Watch Good Love Go Bad)," and Phil wrote "When Will I Be Loved" (later covered note for note by Dave Edmunds and Nick Lowe, two of the brothers' most fervent contemporary admirers). Reunited two years ago, the Everlys are once again busy demonstrating that their powers have yet to peak.

Picking ten acts to enter the first rank of the Rock and Roll Hall of Fame was a daunting task. Persuasive cases could be wheeled out for several other nominees. In the end, these particular masters were inducted because, all critical arguments in favor of their greatness aside, any listing of rock's elite that overlooked one of them would be in some way crucially incomplete.

II. ROCK TAKES ROOT

EDITOR'S INTRODUCTION

In only half a lifetime rock has gone from the "time of true love and innocent pleasure" described by Loder in the previous section to the extreme cynicism and nihilism shown by some new wave rockers of the 80s. Compared to authentic folk traditions, in which musical styles evolve over centuries, this seems to be an extraordinarily rapid aging process. But compared to the speed of American culture in general, in which news events, celebrities, fashions, and social issues magically appear and disappear, it shows rare endurance. In part this is because the music renews itself periodically by returning to the basic elements set in place by the classic rockers. But it is due as well to rock's ability to incorporate elements of other styles. As critic Albert Goldman wrote in 1967, "The Rock Age has assimilated everything in sight, commencing with the whole of American music: urban and country blues, gospel, hillbilly, Western, 'good-time' (the ricky-tick of the twenties), and Tin Pan Alley. It has reached across the oceans for the sounds and rhythms of Africa, the Middle East, and India. It has reached back in time for the Baroque trumpet, the madrigal, and the Gregorian chant; and forward to the future for electronic music and the noise collages of *musique concrete*."

The first practitioners of this kind of playful musical cannibalism were the Beatles, whose rise, fall, and lasting influence are the subject of Jeff Greenfield's *New York Times Magazine* article "They Changed Rock, Which Changed the Culture, Which Changed Us." With the Beatles, rock music stopped being mere entertainment and became something much more subversive— the principal means by which a formerly unfocused group of people suddenly pulled themselves together and generated that vortex of hedonism and social activism that used to be called the counterculture. The version that flourished on the West Coast, where the call to libertinism reached outrageous extremes, is recreated in the second selection, "The Sounds of Silence," an excerpt from Ian Whitcomb's memoir *Rock Odyssey*. The third selection, reprinted from Jim McEwen and Jim Miller's *Rolling*

Stone Illustrated History of Rock and Roll, recounts the development of Motown, acid rock's polar opposite—a smooth, controlled, polished sound that compressed the power of gospel and blues into a strictly regulated formula for radio hits.

The last three articles cover some of the genres of 70s and 80s rock, which has rarely matched 60s rock for sheer passion but far eclipsed it in profitability. Jim Miller's "Some Future" and Kit Rachlis's "Back on the Street Again," reprinted from *New Republic* and *Mother Jones*, examine two such genres, the former among white performers (punk) and the latter among black (rap). In the final selection, a *Time* magazine article, "Songs from the High Ground," Jay Cocks discusses a peculiarly 80s phenomenon: the giant charity concert and best-selling charity record. What is noteworthy about these benefits is the number of performers who donate their services—a sign that benign social activism is in fashion, perhaps because it constitutes a form of free advertising—and the musical spectrum represented by the contributors. The U.S.A. for Africa record, for example, had stars from every genre of rock collaborating on a single song and was sold to consumers from nearly every demographic category. The televised versions of these concerts showed an audience united in enthusiasm for every brand of rock music presented, from whatever era, by whatever performer. Perhaps this can be taken as evidence that the synthetic quality of rock music has finally produced a generation of listeners who are losing their prejudices and can appreciate all kinds of sounds that their forebears were too inhibited to like. A cynic would say that rock has finally succeeded in debasing public tastes to their lowest common denominator, and that rock audiences simply love anyone who is famous.

THEY CHANGED ROCK, WHICH CHANGED THE CULTURE, WHICH CHANGED US[1]

They have not performed together on stage for more than eight years. They have not made a record together in five years.

[1]Reprint of a magazine article by writer Jeff Greenfield. *New York Times Magazine*. p12+. F. 16, '75. Copyright © 1975 by The New York Times Company. Reprinted by permission.

The formal dissolution of their partnership in a London court-room last month was an echo of an ending that came long ago. Now each of them is seeking to overcome the shadow of a past in which they were bound together by wealth, fame and adulation of an intensity unequaled in our culture. George Harrison scorns talk of reunion, telling us to stop living in the past. John Lennon told us years ago that "the dream is over."

He was right: When the Beatles broke up in 1970 in a welter of lawsuits and recriminations, the sixties were ending as well—in spirit as well as by the calendar. Bloodshed and bombings on campus, the harsh realities beneath the facile hopes for a "Woodstock nation," the shabby refuse of counterculture communities, all helped kill the dream.

What remains remarkable now, almost 20 years after John Lennon started playing rock 'n' roll music, more than a decade after their first worldwide conquest, is how appealing this dream was; how its vision of the world gripped so much of a generation; how that dream reshaped our recent past and affects us still. What remains remarkable is how strongly this dream was triggered, nurtured and broadened by one rock 'n' roll band of four Englishmen whose entire history as a group occurred before any of them reached the age of 30.

Their very power guarantees that an excursion into analysis cannot fully succeed. Their songs, their films, their lives formed so great a part of what we listened to and watched and talked about that everyone affected by them still sees the Beatles and hears their songs through a personal prism. And the Beatles themselves never abandoned a sense of self-parody and put-on. They were, in Richard Goldstein's phrase, "the clown-gurus of the sixties." Lennon said more than once that the Beatles sometimes put elusive references into their songs just to confuse their more solemn interpreters. "I am the egg man," they sang, not "egghead."

Still, the impact of the Beatles cannot be waved away. If the Marx they emulated was Groucho, not Karl, if their world was a playground instead of a battleground, they still changed what we listened to and how we listened to it; they helped make rock music a battering ram for the youth culture's assault on the mainstream, and that assault in turn changed our culture permanently. And if the "dream" the Beatles helped create could not sustain itself in the real world, that speaks more to our false hopes than to their

promises. They wrote and sang songs. We turned it into politics
and philosophy and a road map to another way of life. The
Beatles grew up as children of the first generation of rock 'n' roll,
listening to and imitating the music of Little Richard, Larry Williams, Chuck Berry, Elvis Presley, and the later, more sophisticated sounds of the Shirelles and the Miracles. It was the special
genius of their first mentor, Brian Epstein, to package four Liverpool working-class "rockers" as "mods," replacing their greasy
hair, leather jackets and on-stage vulgarity with jackets, ties,
smiles and carefully groomed, distinctive haircuts. Just as white
artists filtered and softened the raw energy of black artists in the
nineteen-fifties, the Beatles at first were softer, safer versions of
energetic rock 'n' roll musicians. The words promised they only
wanted to hold hands; the rhythm was more insistent.

By coming into prominence early in 1964, the Beatles probably saved rock 'n' roll from extinction. Rock in the early nineteen-sixties existed in name only; apart from the soul artists, it
was a time of "shlock rock," with talentless media hypes like Fabi-
an and Frankie Avalon riding the crest of the American Band-
stand wave. By contrast, the Beatles provided a sense of musical
energy that made successful a brilliant public-relations effort. Of
course, the $50,000 used to promote the Beatles' first American
appearance in February, 1964, fueled some of the early hysteria;
so did the timing of their arrival.

Coming as it did less than a hundred days after the murder
of John Kennedy, the advent of the Beatles caught America aching for any diversion to replace the images of a flag-draped casket
and a riderless horse in the streets of Washington.

I remember a Sunday evening in early February, standing
with hundreds of curious collegians in a University of Wisconsin
dormitory, watching these four longhaired (!) Englishmen trying
to be heard over the screams of Ed Sullivan's audience. Their music seemed to me then derivative, pleasant and bland, a mixture
of hard rock and the sounds of the black groups then popular. I
was convinced it would last six months, no more.

The Beatles, however, had more than hype; they had talent.
Even their first hits, "I Want to Hold Your Hand," "She Loves
You," "Please Please Me," "I Saw Her Standing There," had a
hint of harmonies and melodies more inventive than standard
rock tunes. More important, it became immediately clear that the
Beatles were hipper, more complicated, than the bovine rock
stars who could not seem to put four coherent words together.

In the spring of 1964, John Lennon published a book, "In His Own Write," which, instead of a ghost-written string of "groovy guides for keen teens," offered word plays, puns and black-humor satirical sketches. A few months later came the film "A Hard Day's Night," and in place of the classic let's-put-on-a-prom-and-invite-the-TeenChords plot of rock movies, the Beatles and director Richard Lester created a funny movie parodying the Beatles's own image.

I vividly recall going to that film in the midst of a National Student Association congress; at that time, rock 'n' roll was regarded as high-school nonsense by this solemn band of student-body presidents and future C.I.A. operatives. But after the film, I sensed a feeling of goodwill and camaraderie among that handful of rock fans who had watched this movie: The Beatles were media heroes without illusion, young men glorying in their sense of play and fun, laughing at the conventions of the world. They were worth listening to and admiring.

The real surprise came at the end of 1965, with the release of the "Rubber Soul" album. Starting with that album, and continuing through "Revolver" and "Sgt. Pepper's Lonely Hearts Club Band," the Beatles began to throw away the rigid conventions of rock 'n' roll music and lyrics. The banal abstract, second-hand emotions were replaced with sharp, sometimes mordant portraits of first-hand people and experiences, linked to music that was more complicated and more compelling than rock had ever dared attempt. The Beatles were drawing on their memories and feelings, not those cut from Tin Pan Alley cloth.

"Norwegian Wood" was about an unhappy, inconclusive affair ("I once had a girl/or should I say/she once had me"). "Michelle" and "Yesterday" were hauting, sentimental ballads, and Paul McCartney dared sing part of "Michelle" in French—most rock singers regarded English as a foreign language. "Penny Lane" used cornets to evoke the suggestion of a faintly heard band concert on a long-ago summer day. Staccato strings lent urgency to the story of "Eleanor Rigby."

These songs were different from the rock music that our elders had scorned with impunity. Traditionally, rock 'n' roll was rigidly structured: 4/4 tempo, 32 bars, with a limited range of instruments. Before the Beatles, rock producer Phil Spector had revolutionized records by adding strings to the drums, bass, sax and guitar, but the chord structure was usually limited to a basic blues or ballad pattern. Now the Beatles, with the kind of visibility that made them impossible to ignore, were expanding the range of rock, musically and lyrically. A sitar—a harpsichord effect—a ragtime piano—everything was possible.

With the release of "Sgt. Pepper" in the spring of 1967, the era of rock as a strictly adolescent phenomenon was gone. One song, "A Day in the Life," with its recital of an ordinary day combined with a dreamlike sense of dread and anxiety, made it impossible to ignore the skills of Lennon and McCartney. A decade earlier, Steve Allen mocked the inanity of rock by reading "Hound Dog" or "Tutti-Frutti" as if they were serious attempts at poetry. Once "Sgt. Pepper" was recorded, Partisan Review was lauding the Beatles, Ned Rorem proclaimed that "She's Leaving Home" was "equal to any song Schubert ever wrote," and a Newsweek critic meant it when he wrote: "'Strawberry Fields Forever' [is] a superb Beatleizing of hope and despair in which the four minstrels regretfully recommend a Keatsian lotus-land of withdrawal from the centrifugal stresses of the age."

"We're so well established," McCartney had said in 1966, "that we can bring fans along with us and stretch the limits of pop." By using their fame to help break through the boundaries of rock, the Beatles proved that they were not the puppets of backstage manipulation or payola or hysterical 14-year-olds. Instead, they helped make rock music *the* music of an entire international generation. Perhaps for the first time in history, it was possible to say that tens of millions of people, defined simply by age, were all doing the same thing: they were listening to rock 'n' roll. That fact changed the popular culture of the world.

Rock 'n' roll's popularity had never been accompanied by respectability, even among the young. For those of us with intellectual pretenses, rock 'n' roll was like masturbation: exciting, but shameful. The culturally alienated went in for cool jazz, and folk music was the vehicle for the politically active minority. (The growth of political interest at the start of the sixties sparked something of a folk revival).

Along with the leap of Bob Dylan into rock music, the Beatles destroyed this division. Rock 'n' roll was now broad enough, free enough, to encompass every kind of feeling. Its strength had always been rooted in the sexual energy of its rhythms; in that sense, the outraged parents who had seen rock as a threat to their children's virtue were right. Rock 'n' roll made you want to move and shake and get physically excited. The Beatles proved that this energy could be fused with a sensibility more subtle than the "let's-go-down-to-the-gym-and-beat-up-the-Coke-machine" quality of rock music.

In 1965, Barry McGuire recorded the first "rock protest" song (excluding the teen complaints of the Coasters and Chuck Berry). In his "Eve of Destruction," we heard references to Red China, Selma, Alabama, nuclear war and middle-class hypocrisy pounded out to heavy rock rhythms. That same year came a flood of "good time" rock music, with sweet, haunting melodies by groups like the Lovin' Spoonful and the Mamas and the Papas. There were no limits to what could be done; and the market was continually expanding.

The teen-agers of the nineteen-fifties had become the young adults of the nineteen-sixties, entering the professions, bringing with them a cultural frame of reference shaped in good measure by rock 'n' roll. The "youth" market was enormous—the flood of babies born during and just after World War II made the under-25 population group abnormally large; their tastes were more influential than ever before. And because the music had won acceptability, rock 'n' roll was not judged indulgently as a "boys will be boys" fad. Rock music was expressing a sensibility about the tangible world—about sensuality, about colors and sensations, about the need to change consciousness. And this sensibility soon spilled over into other arenas.

Looking back on the last half of the last decade, it is hard to think of a cultural innovation that did not carry with it the influence of rock music, and of the Beatles in particular: the miniskirt, discothèques, the graphics of Peter Max, the birth of publications like Rolling Stone, the "mind-bending" effects of TV commercials, the success of "Laugh-In" on television and "Easy Rider" in the movies—all of these cultural milestones owe something to the emergence of rock music as the most compelling and pervasive force in our culture.

This is especially true of the incredible spread of drugs—marijuana and the hallucinogens most particularly—among the youth culture. From "Rubber Soul" through "Sgt. Pepper," Beatle music was suffused with a sense of mystery and mysticism: odd choral progressions, mysterious instruments, dreamlike effects, and images that did not seem to yield to "straight" interpretation. Whether specific songs ("Lucy in the Sky with Diamonds," "A Little Help From My Friends") were deliberately referring to drugs is beside the point. The Beatles were publicly recounting their LSD experiences, and their music was replete with antirational sensibility. Indeed, it was a commonplace among my contemporaries that Beatle albums could not be understood fully without the use of drugs. For "Rubber Soul," marijuana; for "Sgt. Pepper," acid. When the Beatles told us to turn off our minds and float downstream, uncounted youngsters assumed that the key to this kind of mind-expansion could be found in a plant or a pill. Together with "head" groups like Jefferson Airplane and the Grateful Dead, the Beatles were, consciously or not, a major influence behind the spread of drugs.

In this sense, the Beatles are part of a chain: (1) the Beatles opened up rock; (2) rock changed the culture; (3) the culture changed us. Even limited to their impact as musicians, however, the Beatles were as powerful an influence as any group or individual; only Bob Dylan stands as their equal. They never stayed with a successful formula; they were always moving. By virtue of their fame, the Beatles were a giant amplifier, spreading "the word" on virtually every trend and mood of the last decade.

They were never pure forerunners. The Yardbirds used the sitar before the Beatles; the Beach Boys were experimenting with studio enhancement first; the Four Seasons were using elaborate harmonies before the Beatles. They were never as contemptuously anti–middle-class or decadent as the Kinks or the Rolling Stones; never as lyrically compelling as Dylan; never as musically brilliant as the Band; never as hallucinogenic as the San Francisco groups. John Gabree, one of the most perceptive of the early rock writers, said that "their job, and they have done it well, has been to travel a few miles behind the avant-garde, consolidating gains and popularizing new ideas."

Yet this very willingness meant that new ideas did not struggle and die in obscurity; instead, they touched a hundred million minds. Their songs reflected the widest range of mood of any group of their time. Their openness created a kind of salon for a whole generation of people, an idea exchange into which the youth of the world was wired. It was almost inevitable that, even against their will, their listeners shaped a dream of politics and life-style from the substance of popular music. It is testament both to the power of rock music, and to the illusions which can be spun out of impulses.

The Beatles were not political animals. Whatever they have done since going their separate ways, their behavior as a group reflected cheerful anarchy more than political rebellion. Indeed, as editorialists, they were closer to The Wall Street Journal than to Ramparts. "Taxman" assaults the heavy progressive income tax ("one for you, 19 for me"), and "Revolution" warned that "if you go carrying pictures of Chairman Mao/you ain't gonna make it with anyone anyhow."

The real political impact of the Beatles was not in any four-point program or in an attack on injustice or the war in Vietnam. It was instead in the counterculture they had helped to create. Somewhere in the nineteen-sixties, millions of people began to regard themselves as a class separate from mainstream society *by virtue of their youth and the sensibility that youth produced.*

The nineteen-fifties had produced the faintest hint of such an attitude in the defensive love of rock 'n' roll; if our parents hated it, it had to be good. The sixties had expanded this vague idea into a battle cry. "Don't trust anyone over 30!"—shouted from a police car in the first massive student protest of the decade at Berkeley—suggested an outlook in which the mere aging process was an act of betrayal, in which youth itself was a moral value. Time magazine made the "under-25 generation" its Man of the Year in 1967, and politicians saw in the steadily escalating rebellion among the middle-class young a constituency and a scapegoat.

The core value of this "class" was not peace or social justice; it was instead a more elusive value, reflected by much of the music and by the Beatles' own portrait of themselves. It is expressed best by a scene from their movie "Help!" in which John, Paul, George and Ringo enter four adjoining row houses. The doors open—and suddenly the scene shifts inside, and we see that these "houses" are in fact one huge house; the four Beatles instantly reunite.

It is this sense of communality that was at the heart of the youth culture. It is what we wished to believe about the Beatles, and about the possibilities in our own lives. If there is one sweeping statement that makes sense about the children of the last decade, it is that the generation born of World War II was saying "no" to the atomized lives their parents had so feverishly sought.

The most cherished value of the counterculture—preached if not always practiced—was its insistence on sharing, communality, a rejection of the retreat into private satisfaction. Rock 'n' roll was the magnet, the driving force, of a shared celebration, from Alan Freed's first mammoth dance parties in Cleveland in 1951, to the Avalon Ballroom in San Francisco, to the be-ins in our big cities, to Woodstock itself. Spontaneous gathering was the ethic: Don't plan it, don't think about it, *do* it—you'll get by with a little help from your friends.

In their music, their films, their sense of play, the Beatles reflected this dream of a ceaseless celebration. If there *was* any real "message" in their songs, it was the message of Charles Reich: that the world would be changed by changing the consciousness of the new generation. "All you need is love," they sang. "Say the word [love] and you'll be free." "Let it be." Everything's gonna be all right."

As a state of mind, it was a pleasant fantasy. As a way of life, it was doomed to disaster. The thousands of young people who flocked to California or to New York's Lower East Side to join the love generation found the world filled with people who did not share the ethic of mutual trust. The politicization of youth as a class helped to divide natural political allies and make politics more vulnerable to demagogues. As the Beatles found in their own personal and professional lives, the practical outside world has a merciless habit of intruding into fantasies; somebody has to pay the bills and somebody has to do the dishes in the commune and somebody has to protect us from the worst instincts of other human beings. John Lennon was expressing some very painful lessons when he told *Rolling Stone* shortly after the group's break-up that "nothing happened except we all dressed up . . . the same bastards are in control, the same people are runnin' everything."

He was also being unfair. If the counterculture was too shallow to understand how the world does get changed, the forces that were set loose in the nineteen-sixties have had a permanent effect. The sensuality that rock 'n' roll tapped will never again be bottled up. The vestiges of the communal dream have changed the nature of friendships and life-styles and marriages, in large measure for the better. And with the coming of harder economic times, the idea of abandoning private retreat for shared pleasures and burdens has a direct contemporary practicality.

For me, the final irony is that the Beatles themselves have unconsciously proven the value of communality. As a group, they seemed to hold each other back from excess: McCartney was lyrical, but not saccharine; Lennon was rebellious but not offensive; Harrison's mysticism was disciplined (Ringo was always Ringo, drummer and friend). Now, the sense of control seems to have loosened. Paul and Linda McCartney seem tempted by the chance to become the Steve and Eydie of rock; Lennon is still struggling to free himself from a Fad of the Month mentality; George Harrison's Gospel According to Krishna succeeded in boring much of his audience on his recent concert tour. Perhaps the idea they did so much to spread several years ago is not as dead as all that; perhaps we all need a little help from our friends. The enduring power of that idea is as permanent as any impact their music had on us, even if they no longer believe it.

1966: "THE SOUNDS OF SILENCE"[2]

In San Francisco, the food of the gods was acid. Acid had created those gods from regular (and irregular) folks and now, metamorphosed, they were ready to perform missionary work around the country. For acid wasn't just a private pleasure, it was a revolutionary tool for inspiring within common clay a cornucopia of poems, novels, paintings, and music. Acid could end the war between the three brains; it could unite the world and achieve *Nirvana*. Acid was a crash course in the solution of that age-old occidental problem of *alienation*. LSD said, *"We are one."*

But, looking at the new gods—at the inhabitants of Haight-Ashbury—one could be forgiven for thinking that they appeared very much like bohemians through the ages: the Beats, the Dadaists, the long-haired, wild-eyed avant-garde painters, Oscar Wilde rolling down the Strand with a lily behind the left ear. A harmless weirdness confined to a lunatic few—and in certain neighborhoods. But this latest manifestation was different—for San Francisco's life and lore was to spread throughout America and the

[2]Excerpt from *Rock Odyssey* by Ian Whitcomb. Copyright © 1983 by Ian Whitcomb. Reprinted by permission of Doubleday & Company, Inc.

Western world and was to turn the heads of the Beatles, Stones, and other movers and shakers of rock 'n' roll music. For them, things were never going to be quite the same again. . . .

LSD, hoped the pill pioneers in 1966, would be an elixir that would eventually purify the polluted mainstream. Over the next two years, "Operation LSD" was to find millions of volunteer recruits so that, for a moment, the meandering sidestream of American dissent would actually appear to be flowing into the mainstream itself, flooding shiny, squeaky-clean Main Street, U. S.A. This would constitute a first in American history.

For the Un-Americans, the antijoiners, had never topped any popularity chart before now. They constituted a tiny special-interest group in a land of special-interest groups. The Pilgrim Fathers themselves were one such group. But the antijoiners were true reactionaries because they didn't agree with the nation's dream to become One Big Bloc under the Chief. Though the similarities in language might lead the casual observer to believe that Britain and America were brothers, in fact, the Republic had more in common with the timetable precision and finely structured order of North Germany, in particular the Prussia of the late-nineteenth century. Well-drilled Masses led by the Few. A subtle distinction between Germany and America was that, in the latter, the blocs were treated as if they were sports teams and the whole business was run as if one great game was being played. This made life more fun.

For example, the Constitution was the rule book and pretty rigid in its "do's" and "don'ts." And to be a voter, one had to register. Many colleges, too, had a violent spanking and dehumanizing game as the initiation test. Most aspects of American life were described in terms from organized sport: an original idea was "out of left field," a business venture couldn't even "get to first base," a building contractor's fee was "in the ball park," a lusty bachelor was "playing the field" and might even be a "switch-hitter," for he was known to wear a pink shirt on a Thursday.

The ambition of every red-blooded American was to join the Chief's Brigade, but there was, of course, only room at the top for the tough Few. Anyway, in a game everyone can't be captain. But what was nice in this game was that the captain and his lieutenants were known by their first names and looked just like any Joe. So the head Joe and his shirt-sleeved Jims organized the nation into suckers and con men—the most successful chapter being the crime organization. Early on in the game, the American Fathers had shown a repugnance for democracy—this was a Republic and therefore quite a different matter—and, as late as 1917, U.S. Army manuals described democracy as synonymous with "mobocracy." The Masses were fine, providing they stood in line and paid their admission fee. One of the most shining examples of good business organization was show business: from ragtime to rock 'n' roll, the story had been one of order and conformity, with wild and crazy folk sounds like jazz being soon tamed and packaged by the show business and then—amazingly—sold back to those very suckers who'd created the raw material in the first place!

In contrast, Britain was a loose-knit confederacy of recalcitrant, cantankerous, eccentric curmudgeons. Which was probably why, on the whole, the place simply didn't work very efficiently. Britain was crawling with loonies and loners and so there was no need for current myths starring rugged individualists. Shadowy ancients like Robin Hood and King Arthur would suffice. But in America the rigid two-team conformity demanded a myth opiate and at once. The Wild West provided the heroes. In actuality, the cowboys, trappers, frontiersmen, and bandits had been the bane and bore of the West, the real winners being the solid, hard-working, God-fearing folk who built the towns and stayed in them. But actuality can lead to madness caused by an excess of the mundane and so some of these pesky varmints who had gotten in the way of the real pioneers were called into service as romantic folk heroes, as earnest innocents blazing a lone trail of individuality: Kit Carson, Jesse James, Billy the Kid, etc.

In outlining my theory of Bloc America, I don't mean to put down this ordered neatness. I thoroughly approve, indeed I am envious. To be a member of a group, be it scout troop, football team, or college fraternity, has always been a prime goal for me—but one that has constantly eluded me.

So when I first arrived in the U.S.A. in 1963, I was immediately impressed by the Prussian precision—everything worked and was on time—and by the predilection for uniforms. Everybody seemed to be in glamorous costumes of the musical comedy variety. Even the bagmen at the airports were kitted out like four-star generals. Youth was constantly clicking to attention and barking, "Yes, sir!" to its elders. Even to me. Swimming pools and beaches had guards and posted rules. There were so many "no-no's" in American life. But people seemed to be quite cheerful, brushing their teeth three times a day, driving at the correct speed, eating the same cuisine at chain after chain coffee shop, rooting for the pom-pom girls. I was perfectly content. For the old folkways of black and hillbilly music were not threatened and their existence added a touch of tabasco to the bland consistency of overground America.

However, running parallel with the mainstream was always the sidestream of dissent. It never involved the working classes and it had always been piddling little. The Un-Americans were fired by a fear of machinery and the city. They were usually of an educated-middle-class background, but they liked to disguise this fact by pretending to be "glorious paupers." Herman Melville identified the bohemians of his day as "Painters and sculptors, or indigent students, or teachers of languages, or fugitive French politicians, or German philosophers." But by the 1920s, with post–World War I America swept reasonably clean of aliens, the bohemians were now native Americans and holed up in Greenwich Village, New York, where, amid the usual unmade beds and clogged kitchen sinks, they were free to rail in art against the order surrounding their ghetto. The musically inclined were attracted, at a safe distance, to black jazz because of its furtive and outlaw character.

During the Depression, the bohemians found too much competition from real down-and-outs and the hobby shriveled up and away. But after World War II, when the country made tremendous progress toward a middle-class standard with much upward climbing toward managerial positions and much reading of Emily Post's etiquette book, the bohemian urge took on a new lease of life. Poetry, existentialism, Zen Buddhism, and general slacking were the main features of Greenwich Village life. In music a search was instigated to try and find genuine folk singers, but the more antsy of the New Bohemians went for the stronger meat of modern jazz, of be-bop. They particularly dug Charlie Parker, not just because of the rap flurry of worry notes that flew out of his sax but also because he had headed himself toward autodestruction. The life-style of the cool black hipster was admired and copied by the white bohemians, particularly the slang and the drug usage. Norman Mailer dubbed them "White Negroes" and noted that what they admired had many of the characteristics of the psychopath—the instant satisfaction, the rebellion without cause, the craving to make headlines—and wrote that though it was liberating to be hip ("an instant understanding through intuition") and crazy, "It is not granted to the hipster to grow old gracefully."

The "White Negroes," said Mailer, were a new breed of urban adventurers "drifting out at night, looking for action with a black man's code to fit their facts." Though they had little in common with American intellectuals and arbiters of taste, they did share a *bête noire* of monstrous proportions: Southern white music, all the way from revivalist "Amazing Grace" sway-singing through hillbilly nose ballads to rousing rockabilly. They hated such aberrations with a mighty passion—for they realized that, like respectable black jazz, this music couldn't be separated from its background, which was White Trash, nigger-in-the-woodpile of U.S. social history. The dark white heartland, those full-gospeling, beer-swilling, gun-happy, clog-dancing, guitar-thrashing, frozen-haired primates—the descendants of the indentured servants of the Daughters of the American Revolution—scared them to death. Send Louis Armstrong around the globe as an example of American culture, but put a Band-Aid on the mouth of those nasal whiners from hicksville!

So when Elvis Presley, King of Rock 'n' Roll and triumph of the South, burst on the world like a carbuncle, the deep-thinking minority hoped he was just a passing fancy, another gimmick thrown up by corrupt capitalist show biz, that opiate arm of Big Government. Bop 'n' Folk, with a smidgen of Charles Ives, was their music and the nastier the better. Ironically, the young San Franciscans who were to continue the Un-American tradition would be utilizing rock 'n' roll, Elvis music, albeit filtered through the merry sound of the British Invaders. For the little hipsters—the hippies—had learned their credo and lingo from the local manifestation of Un-Americanism: the beatniks. It was the Beat way of life that was to be role model for the rock generation that was to spread from its San Francisco beginnings all around the country and to certain parts of the world, killing off the old show biz.

For a while, then, we must examine the Beats as hippie-rock mentors. As a group, they had started in the late forties. The founders were all writers: William Burroughs, Jack Kerouac, and Allen Ginsberg. Many of their ideas were based on hipster life, but they were more self-conscious about playing outlaw/misfit because they wrote words whose finality stared back at them like monuments.

Their creed was summed up in the command "*Go*"—which was the favorite expression of their idol, their buddy: Neal Cassady, who boasted the correct Outsider credentials. By the age of twenty-one, he claimed he had stolen 500 cars, screwed 750 chicks, and spent fifteen months in jail. A muscular "rough trade" lug of no fixed address, he wore as his uniform ripped jeans with no underwear and a sausage-skin T-shirt. He was fond of being surprised in the nude. To abolish time was his ambition, but in the meantime he was forever trying to stay ahead of the clock. With mind, body, and desires running at a million m.p.h., he was all "*Go!*" Like any decent psychopath, he believed that the world revolved around his appetites, but he was really at his most characteristic when in transit gloria—stretched out at arm's length behind the wheel of a car roaring bicoastally. He rapped nonstop about how he dug every little detail of crisscross-country America. He was the archetypal outcast, the drifting mechanized cowboy, and the exact opposite of the 1950s uptight gray-flanneled Mr. "Organization Man" Jones of the manicured suburbs or the poorer, paunchy zombie, Mr. Blue Collar of Levittown.

To his writer pals, Cassady, an unschooled boy-man sprite, was a meaty model of Zen Buddhism in action, penetrating beyond the mundane logical mind into the true core of the human spirit. And that spirit—that all-knowing intuition—dictated the message: the only real goal in life was to be constantly celebrating the ecstasy of the passing moment. To stop and consider was to realize the absurdity of the whole game because the Damocles sword of the H-bomb was saying that "Man is nothing" and the past is a foreign country and the future is nonexistent. So it's all "*Go!*" Experience must be pushed to its utmost limits—even as far as the cliff overlooking the valley of death—in order for one to discover one's real nature and thus attain manhood. You are the center of the universe because all else is nonsense, chaos that can't be trusted. But make friends with chaos . . . . Go find the ultimate truth by walking on the wild side of the city late at night—say, in a dingy black bar where the bopper's horn is sending us all heavenward with his jet-propelled blue notes and we get a boost from bennies, bottle, and needle.

Jack Kerouac banged it all down in hot bop prosody. In *On the Road*, a chronicle of the Beat Generation thinly disguised as fiction, he immortalized Cassady as a ramblin' rapper hero. Detailing the picaresque road life in the Other America, the book became a Beat primer and Kerouac became the Hippie Homer. Legend had it that he typed the novel in a trance as one long paragraph on one fat roll of UPI teletype paper. Truth was, that the book went through many rewrites between the first draft in 1951 and the final version published in 1957. No question, though, that *On the Road* was a rich read and a tall adventure that contained many passages that were to inspire hippie life in the swinging psychedelic years just ahead: "The only people for me are the mad ones—mad to live, mad to talk, desirous of everything at the same time."

In 1957, the book spent a long time on the bestseller lists and, by the end of the fifties, Kerouac was an international name, with Ginsberg and Burroughs not far behind. Mass-circulation magazines like *Life* helped spread the word and soon a generation of properly accredited Beats assembled and found a suitable resting place on the penultimate frontier of the West Coast. San Francisco, with its long tradition of radicalism, embracing anarchists, Wobblies, and an independent commercial-free radio network, was most acceptable as an environment. Mysterious fog, magic mountains, and an ocean view looking toward the East, where the brown rice and the answers came from.

The Beats were thickest in North Beach, a cluster of funky coffee houses, bookshops, and clubs, plus attractive low-rent housing, so that the Outsiders were free to hang loose and do their thing in peace. Soon the press was covering this phenomenon, and the Beats were dubbed "beatniks," spaced-out spinoffs from the recent Sputnik. Ginsberg, happy in his long-sought celebrity status, could be seen by the bus-tour patrons shrieking and gesticulating his famous *Howl* poem at smoggy poetry readings to a response of "wows" (boos when he said "Moloch" and cheers when he said "love"). Soon he'd be hitting the college circuit and later there'd be Dylan shows and Beatle stardust.

But for Kerouac, the recognition came too late. Maybe he'd once been an Outsider, way back in the early fifties, but that was only because he'd been left out of the team. As a kid, he'd been a hell of a jock with a bright future, but something had cracked during his service hitch. He was really deeply conservative and

longed to run with the middle boys, but now the pressure was on
the speed-writing champ for more of the same, the crazy *On the
Road* stuff. So he obliged by typing out things like *The Dharma
Bums*—in which lots of the old *On the Road* cast went through the
hoops again, but youth entered as a new element, in a "vision of
a great rucksack revolution, young Americans wandering
around, going up mountains to pray, making children laugh and
old men glad. Zen lunatics—writing poems that happen to appear
in their heads for no reason."

As the sixties opened, the vision came true as thousands of
kids, forsaking the home attractions of the One Big Blue Eye—
the TV—backpacked to Big Sur, Carmel, and San Francisco's
North Beach haunts. They were still a select few, but they were
too many for Kerouac. Dressed as dharma bums, they trekked
even as far as his mother's place in Lowell, Massachusetts, where
they bothered the writer for autographs at the door. But he at
least managed to keep them outside, which was more than he'd
done with Ginsberg, whose beard and garb had scared Mrs.
Kerouac. And even worse were Ken Kesey and his Merry Pranksters, who'd made refrigerator raids, put their feet up on the din-
ing room table, and thrown dinner rolls around indiscriminately.
Kesey should have known better—he'd been a scholar and a real
jock in his time. But these rudenesses, especially the four-letter
words, were too much. And the worst thing was the constant des-
ecration of the American flag, which was later aped by Ginsberg
and Kesey's kid followers. Can't they keep their fiction within a
book? thought Kerouac. Ginsberg was really out to "cash in on the
youth racket," he growled. What the hell was all this fuss about
the Beats anyway? "All we were out for was to get laid," said Jack.
"Look, I may be King of the Beats, but I'm no beatnik!"

By 1964, Kerouac and Ginsberg were among the best-known
American writers in the world. Ginsberg, now fond of wearing
bedsheets in public, went traveling. In Liverpool, he sensed good
vibes, pronouncing the city "the center of the consciousness of
the human universe"; at the Cavern, he was struck by the beautiful boys with their "golden archangelic hair." And on and on he
journeyed, to be feted by French, Dutch, and German youth.
Even the young Turks were lapping up Beat, while back home at
his mother's place, Kerouac watched his once-open road jam up
with an army of spoiled middle-class brats. Their love of dirt and
disorder was hateful and he pinned his hopes on Richard Nixon,

so that things might be set to rights. In his twilight years, Kerouac was a guest on a TV show with hippie spokesman Ed Sanders (leader of the Fugs, specialists in obscene songs). When the neophyte Sanders drooled that *On the Road* had "sparked the hippie movement," Kerouac retorted, "As Buddha said, 'Woe be unto those who spit in the wind—the wind'll blow it back!'"

What really aggravated Kerouac about these hippies was their abuse of hard drugs. A few bennies, a bit of weed, and a slug from the jug were all in a day's work and not out of proportion in a speed-writer's life. But the sixties brats, spoon-fed and Spockmarked, were too lazy to pay their dues, believing that they could get instant Beatitude and become full-fledged artists simply by swallowing tablets of LSD. And this same Ed Sanders had the arrogance to claim: "The drugs are revolutionizing the personalities of individuals, which is the first step in revolutionizing our society and government. I'm for that." Even trendy, youthtrailing Ginsberg admitted that LSD was too strong a potion for him to use as a creative tool.

There was no stopping the rolling stone of Beat gone hippie of the rock movement. Swiss youth, normally placid and sensible, went Beat and Beatle together, for it was thought that they were one and the same, "Yeah! Yeah! Yeah!," "Howl," and "*Go!*" all sounding very similar in a foreign language. What Dr. Albert Hofmann felt about all the hoo-ha is not known. The Swiss chemist, who had invented LSD while working for Sandoz A.G. Laboratories in 1938, had long since dismissed his synthetic concoction as medically useless (he had hoped it might quell migraines) and very harmful if used indiscriminately. Sandoz A.G., learning that many minds were being swiss-cheesed in drughappy America, stopped distributing LSD in the middle sixties, but by that time their patent had run out.

Dr. Hofmann's first LSD trip back in 1943 had been an unusual experience. As he describes it, he was "seized by a peculiar sensation of vertigo and restlessness. . . . With my eyes closed, fantastic pictures of extraordinary plasticity and intensive color seemed to surge toward me." Although he did further experiments with varying dosages, Dr. Hofmann's research was not recreational. A tall stein of lager and a pipe of tobacco were his usual fare. But there was a demand for the hallucinatory drug in America, where they would try anything once. During the war, LSD was tested as a truth serum on prisoners of war (to no effect). Later, it was tried as a tool for discovering the causes of schizophrenia by producing model psychoses (it was certainly good at slivering up the personality for a few mad hours). Perhaps it would work on alcoholics and homosexuals and all the other deviants? At ivory towers on the East and West Coasts, the experiments went on apace and at Harvard a psychology professor named Timothy Leary turned on to the drug as a panacea. For him, LSD was "Eureka!" and the climax of a mind-boggling search that had started for him in Mexico in 1960 when he'd first experienced visions after eating some toasted magic mushrooms.

Suffering from delusions of grandeur, he declared LSD to be the sacrament of a new religion which he would lead as a sexy messiah. His guinea-pig students and fellow researchers were invited to join the new religion and to embark on a world crusade. Leary and Ginsberg (turned on by the professor) had agreed that LSD, by expanding consciousness, could increase people's intelligence and make them better and more beautiful. They resolved to turn the world on to this instant-answer serum: lysergic acid diethylamide or "mysticism by microwave."

News of Leary's experiments reached the Harvard authorities and, when it was learned that the professor was recommending that the U.S. water supply be dosed with LSD so as to be one step ahead of the Russians, they fired him. Now the martyred messiah went on the stump, telling all to "Turn On, Tune In, Drop Out." A stunningly simple slogan, as good as any pop-hit lyric. Never mind that the world as a whole wasn't as bright as Leary, as poetic as Ginsberg, as melodic as Lennon and McCartney, and that this majority would come out of their trips the same plodders as when they went in—*if* they came out intact. Many, of course, were swiss-cheesed for life. Others met death. Unknown millions were to carry the drug around in their system for the rest of their lives, like walking sticks of dynamite ready to go off at any moment. Never mind all these side issues; like all drug users, Leary hated to be alone in his dark deeds: he needed company and he also needed a world congregation for his new religion. Supplied with funds by millionaire benefactors, he set up his church on a large estate in Millbrook, New York, and called his outfit the League for Spiritual Discovery. Soon he had a large flock, including children, and all were gobbling up the acid like there was no tomorrow, which there wasn't.

Leary was a fine propagandist as LSD High Priest, rushing from podium to podium and show to show. He was a great media personality and his pop hook phrase of "Turn On, Tune In, Drop Out" was perfect for easy reading. The authorities could do nothing to stop him because LSD was still legal and would be until October of 1966. But he had little success as High Priest in San Francisco—there were already plenty of gurus in residence and their flocks didn't need to be told about LSD, since their local dope dealers had already unloaded supplies of the latest novelty line. There was even a local manufacturer, Augustus Owsley Stanley III, brewing up a top-grade brand in his own psychedelic spaceship lab. By this time, late 1964, a whole new community based on the magic of LSD was thriving in the Haight-Ashbury district, another low-rent neighborhood like North Beach but full of abandoned Victorian mansions and amenable ethnics whose shops and services came in very handy for the running of the acid village. North Beach, anyway, had been cleaned out earlier in an antibeatnik drive spearheaded by the Italian-Americans and Irish-Catholics. The Haight's eighty-five crumbling blocks were to get a new lease on life and coats of many-colored paints.

Leary was too "hot," too high-handed, too mandarin, and too intellectual for this free-wheeling atmosphere, where the Psychedelic Rangers could be found sharing their acid with Hell's Angels. No, the propagandizing of LSD was in more acceptable hands with Ken Kesey. A wrestling champion and Stanford scholar, Kesey had been an LSD guinea pig at Menlo Park Veteran's Hospital back in the days when Hofmann's mixture was still being tried as a medicine. Like Leary, the experience changed his life, but instead of playing the part of the new messiah he decided to stage-manage a psychodrama roadshow with headquarters in his six-acre estate at La Honda, not far from San Francisco (the funds had come from royalties of his best-selling, drug-induced novel *One Flew Over the Cuckoo's Nest*). At La Honda, there was always a party going on. Kesey had several personae but his favorite was "Mr. Stars and Stripes" and he liked to dress up in a flag suit and do a bit of flag burning on the side.

Visitors to Kesey's circus included the Hell's Angels (who were initiated into acid during a party at the estate), Allen Ginsberg (naturally), and Neal Cassady (whose presence placed the Beat stamp of approval on the whole hedonist enterprise). Determined to scatter the good seed, Kesey often took to the road in a riotously colored magic bus—the first psychedelic (or "magic") bus—crammed with his band of Merry Pranksters and chauffeured by Cassady at full rap. With the refrigerator full of acid-laced orange juice, the performers in different costumes every day, and Captain Trips (Kesey) squatting atop the bus with binoculars around neck and grinning like a demented Rommel, the Prankster entourage must have had the desired shock effect on the decent working people they descended upon.

Back at La Honda, Kesey started throwing a series of parties where the object was to blow the mind on acid—but not quite to smithereens. Those who emerged with a few brain cells intact were the winners, having successfully passed the Acid Test, at a time when America's favorite party game was Charades. These tests got more elaborate and more or less loosely organized, with light shows that featured strobes, funny old silent flicks, endless protoplasms, and slides of dead Indians. Music was provided by a loose group of ex-folkies and avant-garde musicians, recently Dylanized into rock, who called themselves the Grateful Dead. They were most useful at the parties, since they liked to play for free and their numbers had a tendency to go on for two or three hours apiece, enabling the trippers to get through their abysses comforted by suitable acid-rock Muzak.

Together with Jefferson Airplane, the Dead became the most well known of the San Francisco acid-rock bands. Like true jazzmen, they played only when the spirit moved them, so that no sets were ever planned and there was no apparent desire to make the Top Forty. Straight society with its timetables was abhorrent and Chance was all-important—for instance, they'd found the name "Grateful Dead" when a dictionary flipped open to a notation on the burial of Egyptian pharaohs. Their musical roots were coffee-house folk—ancient blues, jug band music, bluegrass, and a touch of Edwardian avant-garde (Charles Ives). Their bass player, Phil Lesh, talked about "bringing Zen consciousness and a polyphonic concept" to their music. Their main spokesman, Jerry Garcia, claimed that "Philosophically, we have nothing to say. We just like to play loud. . . . It's fun to shoot at strangers." The music was very loud, taking its cue from the high-decibeled Yardbirds, and it was mostly blues riffing with tremendous attachment to the drone note, so that the result was a mixture of African and Eastern folk sounds filtered through electronics. The droning, mantralike melody line made Dead music the perfect accompaniment for a trip. Conversely, it could lead to severe headaches if you weren't tripping. One simply had to roll with the flow or get back to Perma-press-ville.

In many ways, the Dead were the children of Beat, living communally and dangerously outside of straight society. The Dead set up their open family in a Haight-Ashbury mansion, where at one time 150 Deadheads could be found living and nearly living. But in other ways, they were different from the Beats, and the main one was in their music: Beats had taken their jazz very seriously and sitting down, with heads bobbing and mouths still except for the occasional "wow" or "outtasight." The Dead and the other acid-rock bands of the Bay Area were into playing music for dancing and partying and this was where they and their fans were to part company with the elder statesmen of Beat. The Acid Tests–turned-dance-parties were attracting thousands of kids who were basically rock fans. Like the local bands, they had come to rock via the Beatles and Stones and now they were proud to have their own local Liverpool with its own sounds, smells, and chemicals.

The Bay, with its burgeoning bands and hungry fans, was ripe for exploitation by entrepreneurs. In the Haight itself, a haphazard start had been made. At one of the rambling old gingerbread mansions-cum-pads—1090 Page Street (twenty-eight rooms and a ballroom)—there had started a series of jam sessions and sometimes actual bands were formed as a result. Big Brother and the Holding Company started here. A fat girl named Janis Joplin would stop by to holler a boozy blues. The Victoriana decor had been hand-painted by members of one of the first Bay bands, the Charlatans. With their hip pizza-parlor straw hats and jug-type music, they weren't about to arouse the rock hungry, but one Chet Helms had been knocked out when he saw them play at a Nevada gig. It gave him the idea for organizing some local dance events, a step beyond the casual jams at Page Street and the arcane frolics in the desert.

Helms was a well-meaning, idealistic soul, very gentle in the true hippie manner. His roommates in another peeling Haight house called themselves the Family Dog and they constituted a kind of village co-op store, with a little dealing in the back room. Helms decided that these jams should become dances at larger local clubs and that the dancers should pay an entrance fee. With this in mind, he went to see local jazz columnist Ralph Gleason—a man over thirty but one who was known to be sympathetic, if not downright excited, by the local band scene.

At home in trenchcoat and tweeds, Gleason was startled by his first sight of Helms and his fellow Family Dogs in their granny glasses, granny dresses, and Sherwood Forest/Wild West gear purchased from the Salvation Army and Goodwill. Helms, shaggy-smiley but firm, announced that L.A. was nothing but a Gomorrah of super-uptight plastic people, then made the proclamation that Family Dog had chosen San Francisco as "the New Liverpool." So would the San Francisco *Chronicle* writer please scour his forty-eight-year-old brain and come up with a cheap-rent locale for their first "dance concert"?

The journalist suggested the Longshoremen's Hall (shades of rip-roaring, radical union days) down at the Fisherman's Wharf. What a crazy idea, bringing the Cuckoo's Nest to San Francisco's very own culinary Disneyland! So in October 1965, the Bay Area rock scene was properly launched at this first Family Dog Dance—entitled "A Tribute to Dr. Strange" (a comic book character). All these dance parties had to seem like spontaneous happenings celebrating something weirdly wonderful and Russ Syracuse, the "All Night Flight" good guy on Top Forty rocker KYA, emceed a bill comprised of Jefferson Airplane, the Great Society, the Marbles, and the Charlatans. Word had been spread by mouth, posters, and radio, and, though these acts were not chartbusters, there was a house fit to bursting. No L.A. act could draw in this manner; it was eerie and exciting. Although the box office did great, the bar business did terribly and, instead of dreary, clinging couple-dancing, there was free-form communal ring-stepping in the Isadora Duncan style with some medieval maypole influence thrown in. The ubiquitous Allen Ginsberg led a Conga line.

Gleason was tickled to death by the colorful turnout and he became an instant convert to Bay Area rock. That same night, at a nearby loft, another older man was experiencing similar feelings as he watched over three thousand people jam into a space that normally might squeeze in six hundred. Bands he'd never heard of blew all night, joined by a stream of players from the Family Dog and other better-known groups. Money was pouring in to swell the coffers of the benefit, which was to aid the San Francisco Mime Troupe. The amazed thirty-six-year-old man was their erstwhile manager, Bill Graham. He saw a percentage in this rocking loft; he saw gleams of a business.

The Mime Troupe were good-time radicals in the Dada vein whose stated goal was to "undermine society" through their street guerrilla theater. Graham had managed as much business as could be mustered—until his patience ran out. He had little sympathy for the griping and pranks of oppressed middle-class kids in a land of plenty. Born Wolfgang Wolodia Grajanka, a Jew, in the Berlin of the 1930s, he'd lost both parents to the gas chambers, but he had managed to escape to the Free World, eventually arriving in New York. Having then toughed his way as a Bronx foster home kid, fought in Korea, gotten a degree in business administration, and finally arrived in 1960s San Francisco as a farm-equipment manufacturer's representative, Bill Graham—filled with all-American business zeal and scarred by European suffering—wasn't about to go wet, woolly, and lovey-dovey with the babes who'd never been bombed—by bombs, that is.

He wanted to stage more benefits and Gleason suggested he rent a bashed-up ballroom in the black ghetto that nudged the Haight. On December 10, 1965, the line to see Jefferson Airplane, the Great Society, and a host of other bands went around the block and beyond. The Fillmore Auditorium made up for its dilapidation with an abundance of space and atmosphere. This could be a groovy—and profitable—environment.

Graham had also booked the Family Dog to perform, so slight was his knowledge of the music game, but Chet Helms soon advised him of his error and the disparate pair were soon in demand as promoters of benefits, dances, and happenings, as heads who could get it all together with no Big Time vibes. When Ken Kesey decided to stage a gargantuan multimedia three-day circus to be called the Trips Festival, Graham was invited to handle the details.

The Trips Festival, in January 1966, marked the culmination of the carefree, hang-loose salad days, the end of psychedelic isolation, and the start of the mass circulation of the news that San Francisco was "where it was all happening." Gleason noted that rock 'n' roll had at last "come of age," implying that the Stone Age of hillbilly beaters and shiny-suited kid crooners was done with. This was the Rock Revolution. Kesey saw his festival as marking a Neon Renaissance and a New Reality, "a new way to look at the world," since the rotten old one was "riddled with radioactive poison." Graham was trying to make sure that the doors of the Longshoremen's Hall were secured, that there were suitable fire escapes, and that the hard drugs were kept hidden.

In effect, the festival was to be an Acid Test without the acid. The multimedia machinery would simulate a trip to *Nirvana* and, if you came a bit stoned, so much the smoother. Over twenty thousand people in a rainbow assortment of fancy dress and arriving in hand-painted, psyched-out cars modeled after the Kesey "magic" bus were to attend, drawn by a bill headed by Kesey and the Merry Pranksters, together with Beatles readings, "the Endless Explosion," "the God Box," Hell's Angels, the vaudeville of Neal Cassady, the music of the Grateful Dead and Big Brother and the Holding Company, and personal appearances by Marshall (*The Media Is the Message*) McLuhan and, of course, Allen Ginsberg. The latter two, surprisingly, were no-shows, but no matter, because the audience had really come to trip on the music and themselves. The Grateful Dead were a huge success, stretching their version of "In the Midnight Hour" until, it seemed, well past breakfast. As for the slide show depicting the plight of the forgotten Indians; "the God Box," in which stoned freaks could bellow over the P.A. about how their heads were expanding on brown rice; and Neal Cassady's vaudeville show of swinging stupidly and dangerously out from the balcony on a rope—it was all the same old stuff to the locals and only the out-of-towners and the press hadn't witnessed such goings on before. Tom Wolfe, outdressed for a change, scribbled away in the men's room.

A silver spaceman kept running around maniacally, stopping to congratulate a fellow freak on his costume, and at one point getting into a nasty row with a tribe of black bongo players who refused to cease and desist: "OK, we've known about all that for three thousand years—but we're now into something *new!*" His tunnel vision did not take in moldy-fig, old-fashioned bongo music. When he later flung open a door to allow a flood of outsiders in for free, the spaceman was in trouble. Graham flew at him in a fury. The silver spaceman pulled off his helmet and grinned idiotically. Of course! It was Kesey himself, in disguise because he was out of jail on probation. Musn't let the fuzz find him at the festival because in court he presents himself as "Mr. Super-Straight Preppy."

There was never any doubt that the whole multimedia simulated drug trip thing was Kesey's creation. He'd pioneered strobes, ectoplasmic slide shows, all the tricks that were to be copied in light shows worldwide. Trouble was, he really didn't understand the power of the music, didn't grow with it—but what was much worse, he was an anarchist. He wasn't organized. The Trips Festival, in Graham's eyes, was an insurance broker's and fire marshal's nightmare. This zoo must be caged and TCB (taking care of business) was the order of the day in the future.

From February on, after the Trips Festival, Graham set the dance-hall scene to rights as a business and the first move he made was to take out a lease on the Fillmore Auditorium. The object was to provide a freak's paradise, complete with multimedia trappings and stacks of bands and macrobiotic refreshments, so that the public started their experience the moment they entered the hall and finished it only when they stepped outside back into banality. *But* Graham also took care of business by having an efficient staff to take the money, clean the toilets, post the signs that forbade illegal doings in hang-loose lingo, and bounce the occasional troublemaker. And though the Graham Organization looked to all appearances like part of the tribe, they were nevertheless inheritors of the Barnum & Bailey legacy. Over at the Avalon Ballroom, the altruistic Chet Helms was operating like a clergyman: he was letting them in for free more often than not. He was dispensing the love dream. When it became obvious that Graham was coining in the loot and was well on the way to becoming a millionaire via his dance concert promotions and his management of groups such as Jefferson Airplane, he was accused of being a "rip-off artist." To this he answered: "I don't sell love—I sell talent and environment." Why should he hold back a pop-music development that he could fit into a swell niche in the Grand Order of American Entertainment?

The next obvious step was to spread this new rock around the country—and this could only be done through hit records. There were no labels to speak of in the Bay Area—only Autumn Records (owned by local concert promoter and ex–Top Forty deejay "Big" Tom Donahue), which was in financial trouble. A year back, they'd had great national success with a local group, the Beau Brummels, who'd hit the Top Twenty twice with "Laugh Laugh" and "Just a Little"—but Autumn didn't have the national distribution to sustain the act. Anyway, the Beaus were at the tail end of a curious American craze for British Invader impersonators.

Of the new acid-rock bands, the one that looked most likely to succeed was Jefferson Airplane. Marty Balin, a foxy ex-dancer and sharp-as-a-pin wielder of a large vocabulary, had been running his own club, the Matrix, where he and the Airplane performed a noticeably tidier and more melodic music than the open-ended wanderings of the Grateful Dead. Like the Dave Clark Five, they could be expected to turn up to a benefit or dance concert or Trips Festival *on time*. Graham was impressed and offered them his management; Gleason trumpeted the band in his column. RCA took note, came up to San Francisco, and signed them, making Jefferson Airplane the first Bay Area band to sign with a major label. The L.A.-produced records that resulted were crisp, clean, and rather sterile—a state-of-the-art sound that RCA engineers had spent years perfecting and one perfect for middle-of-the-road music but quite wrong for displaying Jefferson Airplane in flight. How did you capture all the swirling colors and sweet aroma of the acid dream on plain old vinyl? This was to be a continuing problem for the marketers of the New Sound. Despite this overall blandness of production, the RCA staff and Jefferson Airplane would have two Top Ten singles, "White Rabbit" and "Somebody to Love," and a number-three album, *Surrealistic Pillow,* within the next year.

RCA would certainly have liked to sign up more bands in the fecund Bay Area, but the Colonel refused. No rock 'n' roll outfit was to threaten the throne of his boy Elvis. Sign any more rockers and he would take the boy away—and *bang* goes the company! On the other hand, Warner Bros. Records were hungry indeed. Since their start in the late fifties, they'd been associated with ritzier middle-of-the-road music, light folk music, and comedy. Alan Sherman, Trini Lopez, Dean Martin, and Peter, Paul, and Mary were their stars. Of course, Frank Sinatra (who'd founded Reprise) was a good prestige name, but he was known to detest rock 'n' roll and had even once ordered that there was to be none of that trash on Reprise.

However, Warner Bros./Reprise executives couldn't help but notice that this year's R&R sales figures looked as though they would be 80 percent over 1964 and that, if the trend continued, rock record grosses would be in excess of 25 million units. Early in 1966, a rock record by, of all people, Nancy Sinatra had crashed up to number one ("These Boots Are Made for Walkin'"). A few months later, Warner Bros./Reprise would be surprised by their number seven hit by the Association and even more surprised to learn that the song, "Along Comes Mary," was accused of referring to Mary Jane or marijuana. The company had always been strictly suit and tie. On special occasions, the men would parade in their blue company blazers and it was quite a sight for sore eyes when they marched down the aisle at sales conferences to the music of John Philip Sousa.

But the writing was on the wall—and it was in the form of a psychedelic poster. Joe Smith, general manager of the Warner Bros. half, had already been advising Tom Donahue up at Autumn. The next step was to purchase the ailing but potentially hit-bound company. Tom told Joe that he simply must come up and soak in the scene for himself. So Joe made forays, always careful to dress in his usual Ivy League style (he was a Yale man). He witnessed the Grateful Dead in action at Chet Helms's Avalon Ballroom, staunchly standing through the intoxicating smoke and nodding politely when Helms informed him that the under-twenty-fives were now the majority nationwide and not to trust anyone over thirty. Donahue was around as well, urging Smith to sign up the Dead. "This is where the music's going," he said. Smith replied, "I don't think Jack Warner will ever understand this." But he remembered that Warner and his Bros. had had the vision (or the gambler's instinct) to back talking pictures in 1927 when they went with *The Jazz Singer* and he knew that the bottom line for Warner Bros./Reprise was written "R&R." Therefore, bracing himself to his task and keeping in mind—as a onetime disc jockey—that anything goes in the crazy music biz, he ventured into the tribal commune mansion of the Dead. They tried hard, oh so hard, to get Smith to take some acid, but he resisted and lived to return to L.A. to tell his fellow executives that this new rock was worth a shot. He didn't have to work very hard to persuade them: Mo Ostin, head of Reprise and the man who had once had to carry out Sinatra's antirock policy, had already signed a fiery black guitarist who was shaking them up in England—Jimi Hendrix.

And so it was that the Un-Americans, now settled in San Francisco, got the chance to become a moveable feast on vinyl and in concert. Thus the hippies were invited to join the mainstream of American pop. The question was: would they join the tradition and TCB? Or were they revolutionaries who would turn this neat little America of super salesmanship upside down so that the moon would never shine in June again?

MOTOWN[3]

Sandwiched among a row of modest private homes and professional enterprises like Sykes Hernia Control and Your Fair Lady Boutique and Wig Room, the white bungalow at 2648 West Grand Boulevard in Detroit is distinguished only by a large sign proclaiming it HITSVILLE, U.S.A. The two-story frame structure with the angular, jutting picture window, along with a cluster of nearby houses, is the home of Berry Gordy's Motown Records, currently the country's hottest hit-makers.

Shortly after 9 a.m. on a warm morning in June 1965, songwriter/producer Lamont Dozier strolls in, ignoring the company time clock that used to govern his paycheck. Company president Gordy rushes from his office to tell Lamont that Motown needs a quick followup to the Four Tops' "I Can't Help Myself," the label's second Number One pop hit in less than a month (Dozier had helped write and produce the other as well: the Supremes' "Back in My Arms Again"). The Tops had recorded for Columbia before their Motown association, and Gordy explains that the New York label has just released an old record in an attempt to cash in on the group's current success.

Dozier nods and walks down the corridor, past closet-sized offices where groups and producers rehearse material. Lamont's partners, Brian Holland and Eddie Holland, are already in their cubicle, sketching out a preliminary arrangement that bears more than a passing resemblance to the Four Tops' current smash. Lamont Dozier sits down at the piano and smooths out some rough edges in the melody line; all three contribute to the lyric. By noon the song is complete, and the trio take their finished work to the studio, where the Four Tops run down the lyrics while Earl Van Dyke's band negotiates the changes. Later that afternoon, the track will have been recorded and the Tops' voiceover added. Within three days, the record will be on the streets, the pick hit at local soul station WCHB. The Columbia disc is quickly forgotten, and by August "It's the Same Old Song" by the Four Tops hits Number Five on the *Billboard* pop chart.

[3]Reprint of a chapter by Jim McEwen and Jim Miller. From THE ROLLING STONE ILLUSTRATED HISTORY OF ROCK AND ROLL, by Jim Miller. Copyright ©1976 by Rolling Stone Press. Reprinted by permission of Random House, Inc.

The success of Motown Records is almost entirely attributable to one man: Berry Gordy. A former boxer and onetime record-store owner, Gordy, through a combination of pugnacious panache, shrewd judgment and good taste, became the mogul of the most profitable black music concern in the world.

It all began in Detroit in the early Fifties. When Gordy's record store specializing in jazz went bankrupt, he decided to redirect his musical moneymaking interests to the burgeoning field of rhythm and blues. While supporting himself with a series of odd jobs, Gordy began writing songs for local R&B acts. At first, his amateur efforts failed miserably; but he soon acquired a local reputation as a songwriter, producer and hustler. In those days, Gordy would write songs for a performer, cut a demo tape, and then take the finished master to New York, where he would try to peddle his product for a five percent royalty on net sales. Unfortunately, even when somebody purchased his masters, they were never promoted properly; and if they did sell, royalties were rarely accounted for.

It was a tough racket, but Gordy persevered. His first break came in 1957 when Brunswick Records bought a song he had written, called "Reet Petite," for Jackie Wilson. "Reet Petite" was a pop hit, and though his profit only amounted to $1000, several successful followups for Wilson and Brunswick soon established Berry Gordy as Detroit's leading songwriter. But that was not enough: Gordy was determined to produce and market his own music himself.

The Motown mythology has it that Berry Gordy, fresh off an automobile assembly line, borrowed $700 to start his company. In truth, by 1959 Gordy was a prospering songwriter; he first borrowed money, not to start a label, but to go into independent production.

At the time, he had his eye on a local singer named Marv Johnson. Their first joint effort, "Come to Me," was leased to United Artists; although it was only a modest hit (Number 30 on the pop charts), it gave an indication of where Gordy was headed.

The song itself was slight: simple lyrics set to a stock rock chord progression (compare Gordy's smash hit for Wilson, "Lonely Teardrops"). But to accompany Johnson, who followed in the gospel footsteps of Clyde McPhatter and Wilson, Gordy added a churchy female chorus for some call-and-response trades (shades of Ray Charles), and a bubbling male bassman (shades of

Clyde McPhatter's "A Lover's Question" on Atlantic). Instrumentally, the record was anchored by a persistent baritone sax and tambourine, with a flute break in the middle (recalling Bobby Day's "Rockin-Robin"). The result was a clean R&B record that sounded as white as it did black.

Gordy perfected this gospel-pop fusion in the months that followed, and by 1960 he'd made two similarly styled Top Ten hits with Johnson, "You Got What It Takes" and "I Love the Way You Love." After leasing yet another hit single, "Money" by Barrett Strong, to Anna, a label owned by his sister, Gordy decided to form his own label: Tammie, soon changed to Tamla Records.

It wasn't surprising that the first Tamla hit of any size belonged to a vocal group called the Miracles. Gordy had discovered the quintet working in Detroit; although initially attracted by the group's only female member, Claudette—the lead singer's girlfriend—Gordy quickly realized the potential of the Miracles' songwriter, Smokey Robinson, who also happened to be the lead singer. He leased a few Miracles sides to Chess Records in 1959, but it was only with "Way Over There" on Tamla in 1960 that the group (and label) began to sell records: 60,000 on that release. In a few months, that would seem like chicken feed.

As a followup to "Way Over There," Robinson came up with a song called "Shop Around." Gordy found the first master too sluggish and called the Miracles back into the studio at three o'clock one morning to cut a new version at a faster tempo. The result was Tamla's first real hit; by January, "Shop Around" had reached Number Two on the pop charts, and Gordy's company was in the black.

The little bungalow on West Grand was teeming with activity as a host of aspiring local singers and songwriters flocked to Gordy's studio. With Robinson and Gordy handling the bulk of composing and producing, Tamla and Gordy's growing family of labels (Motown and Gordy were formed in the next two years, later to be joined by Soul, V.I.P. and Rare Earth) began to log an impressive track record, their hits ranging from Eddie Holland's slick "Jamie" to the Contours' rauchy "Do You Love Me." By the end of 1962, the Gordy roster included Mary Wells, the Marvelettes and Marvin Gaye.

Although several of these acts, particularly Mary Wells and the Marvelettes, made consistent inroads onto the pop charts, Motown's early productions differed markedly in feel and appeal, depending on who was doing the singing. Mary Wells cooed seductive lyrics, the Marvelettes declaimed the "girl group" sound, while Marvin Gaye and the Contours both rasped over rotgut rhythm tracks only one step removed from rural blues and gospel. Motown had hits, all right; but it hadn't quite yet evolved a distinctive sound.

From the beginning, Berry Gordy relied on a handful of dependable writers and producers. In late 1961, he began to expand his staff of writer/producers, and among the new additions was Lamont Dozier, a veteran of the local group scene who toiled in relative anonymity at Motown for a couple of years until he began a creative partnership with Motown cohorts Brian and Eddie Holland. In 1963 the fledgling trio of writers clicked. Working with Martha and the Vandellas, the Holland-Dozier-Holland team set out to refine and systematize the production techniques Gordy had pioneered with Marv Johnson. "Heat Wave," by Martha and the Vandellas inaugurated a three-year stretch that saw H-D-H amass 28 Top 20 pop hits.

As soul producers, they were little short of revolutionary. The trio rarely used standard song forms, opting instead for a simpler, more direct *ababcc* pattern, anchored by an endless refrain of the song's hook line. The effect of this cyclical structure was cumulative, giving records produced by Holland-Dozier-Holland a compulsive momentum; even better, the constant refrains and consistent use of repetition helped make their hits ubiquitous: after you'd heard one, you'd heard them all—and each and every one of them was immediately familiar, subtly distinctive and quite unforgettable.

Lyrically, the H-D-H hits were nothing to write home about. But what mattered was their sense of structure, and the musical devices the trio used to animate that structure. Following Gordy's lead, they exploited gospelish vocal gestures in a pop context, now defined by their own streamlined approach. If the vocalists provided emotion, the band mounted a nonstop percussive assault highlighted by a "hot" mix, with shrill, hissing cymbals and a booming bass—anything to make a song jump out of a car radio. With tambourines rattling to a blistering 4-4 beat, the H-D-H sound, introduced on "Heat Wave" and perfected on records like the Four Tops' "Reach Out I'll Be There" and the Supremes' "You Can't Hurry Love" (both from 1966), came to epitomize what Motown would call "The Sound of Young America."

"Heat Wave" and the arrival of Holland-Dozier-Holland kicked Motown into high gear. By the late Sixties, Gordy's company had become one of the biggest black-owned corporations in America, as well as one of the most phenomenally successful independent recording ventures in the history of the industry. Motown succeeded beyond anyone's wildest expectations, and did so with black people controlling the company at the technical and business as well as musical and artistic levels.

The reasons behind Motown's popularity are diverse. Overseeing the whole operation was Berry Gordy, who endorsed the old bromide for predictable success: keep it simple. Under his tutelage, Motown's musicians took the concept of formula pop to a new level of sophistication and, thanks to the music's gospel/blues roots, visceral intensity.

The formulas might have quickly become tedious, of course, were it not for the ingenuity of Gordy's stable of producer/songwriters. Smokey Robinson, who handled the Temptations and Mary Wells in addition to the Miracles, was able to transfigure the most banal romantic motifs with clever lyrics and catchy hook lines; Norman Whitfield, who worked extensively with the Temptations as well as Marvin Gaye and Gladys Knight, was able to go beyond R&B clichés with punchy melodies and arrangements; such latecomers as Nickolas Ashford and Valerie Simpson, who produced the Marvin Gaye–Tammi Terrell duets as well as Diana Ross's solo records, were able to amplify secularized gospel lyrics with grandiose orchestra settings; and finally Holland-Dozier-Holland did nothing less than make The Formula a work of art in itself.

And then there was the Motown house band, an unheralded lot of the best R&B musicians in the Sixties. While Booker T. and the MGs helped define the style of Memphis soul, their largely anonymous Motown counterparts were expected to play only what they were told to play. As a result, the Motown rhythm section, which included the late Benny Benjamin on drums, James Jamerson on bass, Joe Messina on guitar, Earl Van Dyke on keyboards, the late James Giddons on percussion and Robert White on guitar, developed a unique dexterity and adaptability; yet a player like Jamerson nonetheless left his own mark on the music (the explosive bass line on Marvin Gaye and Tammi Terrell's "Ain't No Mountain High Enough" could have come from no one else). Their existence was hardly glamorous, however. Usually paid a flat salary, the Motown musicians toiled in obscurity; where Booker T. and the MGs cut instrumental hits, Earl Van Dyke and the Soul Brothers played small lounges near West Grand for a few dollars, free pizza and the applause of local patrons. In the morning, it was back to the nine-to-five grind.

Indeed, the assembly-line atmosphere had something to do with Motown's success; if nothing else, it enabled Berry Gordy to keep tabs on his empire. He called his direction "quality control"; often, second-string Motown acts would have virtually no public exposure for months at a time while their recordings were polished to Gordy's satisfaction.

Even popular performers found themselves restricted as well as aided by the Motown hit machine. Gordy's innate caution dictated followups that only slightly altered the elements of the previous hit; a formula was minded until it was commercially exhausted. Thus "Heat Wave" reached Number Four on the pop charts; its soundalike successor, "Quicksand," got up to Number Eight—and only after the third go-around, when "Live Wire" stalled at Number 42, did Martha and the Vandellas get the opportunity to try something different.

Gordy's cultivation of Motown's image was equally restrictive. As soon as the company domination of Top 40 pop and soul was clear, Gordy hustled his star acts into "class" venues like the Copa, the Latin Casino, Las Vegas or bust. As if to confer respectability upon his artists, he encouraged albums such as *The Four Tops on Broadway* and *Temptations in a Mellow Mood*. Finally, Gordy devised something called "International Talent Management Incorporated" (I.T.M.I.), a kind of finishing school for Motown stars. I.T.M.I. taught a person how to sit, walk, talk and even how to smoke a cigarette with grace and elegance. Above all, it taught Motown's flock the good manners any adult member of the white middle class would expect to see exhibited at a swank nightclub.

Motown's roots may have been in gospel and blues, but its image was purely one of upward mobility and clean, wholesome fun (Gordy's vision of "Young America"). Motown's stars were groomed to offend no one; the songs they sang were equipped with romantic lyrics that could appeal to practically anyone; and the music itself was rarely demanding, or even aggressive in the tradition of Southern soul. Martha and the Vandellas' "Dancing in the Street" (1964) may have been interpreted by black activist/poet LeRoi Jones as an evocation of revolutionary times, but the

closest thing to an overt political statement released by Motown
in the mid-Sixties was Stevie Wonder's "Blowin' in the Wind"
(1966). (Of course, ever sensitive to changing fashion, Motown
eventually hopped on the political—and even psychedelic—
bandwagon, with hits like the Temptations' "Psychedelic Shack,"
1970, and Edwin Starr's "War," 1970, both Norman Whitfield
compositions.)

One statistic gives eloquent testimony to Gordy's success in
courting the white market. In 1966, Motown's "hit ratio"—the
percentage of records released to make the national charts—was
nothing less than 75%. It was an appropriately awesome achievement for a truly astonishing record company.

Although its hits have occasionally been dismissed on grounds
of monotony, the truth of the matter is that Motown, even in its
assembly-line prime, released a remarkably diverse lot of records,
varying in sound, arrangement and feel. While Berry Gordy dictated the overall direction, and the producers and studio musicians stamped the sound, it was the performers themselves who
ultimately conveyed the Motown image. Here is a brief guide to
the artists who sang the Motown hits (omitting Stevie Wonder,
who is discussed elsewhere):

Miracles. Most of Motown's roster consisted of Detroit acts un-
earthed at local talent shows; here as elsewhere, Smokey Robinson's Miracles set the pattern. When Robinson first approached
Gordy late in 1957, most of the group was still in high school;
three years later, when "Shop Around" hit, the Miracles' oldest
member was barely 21.

During the next ten years, however, the Miracles became a
seasoned troupe, while Robinson became one of the most prolific
and popular producer/songwriters in the Motown stable. In person, the Miracles' performances were erratic, depending on the
state of Smokey's fragile falsetto; by the end of a particularly gru-
eling night, Robinson's voice, always so pure and controlled on
record, often sounded frayed. In the studio, on the other hand,
Robinson knew few rivals, composing and producing such torchy
soul/pop hits as Mary Wells's "My Guy" (1964), the Temptations'
"My Girl" (1965), and the Marvelettes' "The Hunter Gets Captured by the Game" (1967).

Smokey was his own best interpreter, and the Miracles remained one of Motown's most consistent groups throughout the

Sixties. At the outset, their chief asset was the anguished eroticism conveyed by Robinson's pristine falsetto (listen to "You Can
Depend on Me," from 1960). But by the mid-Sixties, Robinson
had also blossomed as a composer and lyricist. As writer Charlie
Gillett has pointed out, many of his finest lyrics hinged on an apparent contradiction: "I'm a choosy beggar," "I've got sunshine
on a cloudy day," "The love I saw in you was just a mirage." Despite a spat of uptempo hits, from "Shop Around" and "Mickey's
Monkey" (1963) to "Going to a Go-Go" (1965), the Miracles' forte
was ballads. Here Robinson—whether confessing his dependence, as on "You've Really Got a Hold on Me" (1962), or pleading for forgiveness, as on "Ooo Baby Baby" (1965)—could use his
voice to transcendent effect. "The Tracks of My Tears" (1965)
remains one of the most emotionally demanding Motown singles
of the Sixties.

Mary Wells. Just 17 when she auditioned for Berry Gordy in
1960, Mary Wells debuted on Motown with "Bye Bye Baby," a
brassy, unrefined shouter. But she didn't really click until early
1962, after she was placed under Smokey Robinson's wing. Their
partnership produced four Top Ten pop hits over a two-year
span, including "The One Who Really Loves You" and "Two
Lovers" (both 1962). A soft, cuddly stylist with just a hint of sassi-
ness, Wells exited Motown shortly after her 21st birthday, lured
by a lucrative contract with another label. Although her departure followed her biggest Motown hit ever, "My Guy" (1964), she
proved unable to duplicate her success elsewhere.

Marvelettes. Motown's first and only real "girl group" was its
most mysterious. Originally a quintet with Gladys Horton as lead,
the Marvelettes survived numerous personnel, production and
stylistic changes for almost a decade. Although the group was a
consistent frontliner only in 1962, when "Please Mr. Postman"
and "Playboy" both made the Top Ten, their repertoire of later
hits included such gems as Smokey Robinson's suave "Don't Mess
with Bill" (1966).

Martha and the Vandellas. Martha Reeves began her career at
Motown inauspiciously enough, as a secretary in the A&R depart-
ment. But Berry Gordy, realizing he had talent sitting right under
his nose, sent Martha to work singing with her own group, the
Vandellas. They debuted as the backup vocalists for Marvin Gaye
on "Stubborn Kind of Fellow," and hit their stride with "Heat
Wave" in 1963. Thanks to Reeves's aggressive and flamboyant

style, the Vandellas escaped any categorization as an orthodox "girl group"; instead, they recorded some of the toughest mainline rock and roll to come out of Motown.

Reeves's main problem was one of excess, but Holland-Dozier-Holland wrote lyrics that successfully capitalized on her shrillness: if her love wasn't like a "Live Wire," then she was falling in "Quicksand." Martha spurned, on the other hand, tended to sound forlorn or cross (as on "Love [Makes Me Do Foolish Things]," from 1965). The best Vandellas records were made with H-D-H; but after the atypically infectious "Jimmy Mack" in early 1967, the two teams went their separate ways. The result for Martha and the Vandellas was little short of disastrous. After 1967, the group never made the Top 40 again.

Marvin Gaye. A stage-shy performer who originally fancied himself a jazz singer, Marvin Gaye has been one of Motown's most enigmatic—and consistently popular—acts. First employed by Gordy as a session drummer, he debuted as a vocalist in 1962 with the herky-jerky "Stubborn Kind of Fellow," and proceeded to work with practically every producer in the Motown stable. With Holland-Dozier-Holland, he made "Can I Get a Witness" (1963), a rough-and-tumble gospel/blues track, and "How Sweet It Is (to Be Loved by You)" (1964), a medium-tempo shouter; with Smokey Robinson, he made "I'll Be Doggone" and "Ain't That Peculiar" (both 1965), two of Smokey's most compelling uptempo productions; with Norman Whitfield he made his historic "I Heard It through the Grapevine" (1968), an extraordinarily sophisticated record that nevertheless seemed to go back a good 400 years for the sources of its dark, utterly ominous incantations ("voodoo music," guitarist Mike Bloomfield once called it). Later, with Ashford and Simpson, Gaye cut a memorable series of duets with the late Tammi Terrell, including "Your Precious Love" (1967) and "You're All I Need to Get By," both majestic, massively orchestrated affirmations of eternal love.

Always one of Motown's most idiosyncratic talents, Gaye entered into a second phase of his career in 1971, with the release of *What's Going On,* a self-composed and -produced song cycle that marked a liberation from Gordy's studio system. (Gaye had previously shown his skill as a songwriter as coauthor of "Dancing in the Streets," and as a writer/producer with the Originals, who cut two gloriously anachronistic hits, "Baby, I'm for Real," 1969, and "The Bells," 1970—both of which betray Gaye's past; he was

once a member of the Moonglows, a vintage Fifties vocal group.)
Songs like "What's Going On" and "Mercy Mercy Me (the
Ecology)" captured a pensive and introspective Gaye, who managed to express the tentative and confused aura of the period; this
strain in his work reached its peak with the magnificent "Inner
City Blues" (also 1971), which featured a hushed, almost damned
sound. Perhaps to cap his career, Gaye followed his more political
work with a return, not to "love," but to pure eroticism, with the
irresistible "Let's Get It On" (1973), a huge hit with some claim
to being the sexiest record Motown ever produced.

Jr. Walker and the All Stars. The sole instrumental star at Motown was Jr. Walker, a veteran of Fifties R&B from Indiana. A
gruff but lyrical tenor saxophonist, he specialized in sustained
high wails, and his sense of timing was impeccable. Walker's early
Motown hits leaned heavily on these instrumental signatures.
With a minimum of production, "Shotgun" (1965) established his
preeminence as a specialist in hot party discs. Gradually, however, Walker was integrated into the Motown system and encouraged to sing more. An affably raspy vocalist, he performed
splendidly on the Holland-Dozier-Holland remake of "How
Sweet It Is (to Be Loved by You)" (1966), then cut several string-
laden hits, including "What Does It Take (to Win Your Love)"
(1969), his last foray into the Top Ten.

Four Tops. Lamont Dozier recalls idolizing the Four Tops in
the late Fifties, when the Detroit group was vacillating between
R&B and a more sedate Mills Brothers style. He admired the
quartet for its professionalism, but above all for its class. Almost
five years later the Tops came to Motown. After an early attempt
at making the group into bona fide supper-club singers, Holland-
Dozier-Holland resurrected the Tops with a sharp midtempo
plea called "Baby I Need Your Loving" (1964).

Built around lead singer Levi Stubbs's dramatic, piercing vocal delivery, the Tops/H-D-H hits came nonstop for almost four
years. Records like " I Can't Help Myself" (1965) and "Reach Out
I'll Be There" (1966) perfectly captured the mid-Sixties Motown
sound: tambourines clapped on the off-beat, drummers pounded
out indelicate 4-4 rhythms, and imaginative horn and string
charts swirled above. Somewhere in the middle was Stubbs, hol-
lering, cajoling and pleading with unflagging intensity. When
Holland-Dozier-Holland left Motown, the group fell on hard
times. The limitations of Stubbs's voice became increasingly ap-

parent, and, after fitful success, the Tops joined the growing exodus from Motown in the early Seventies.

Temptations. While the Four Tops covered the frenetic side of the Motown sound, and the Miracles monopolized its romantic side, the Temptations quite simply stood as the finest vocal group in Sixties soul: they could outdress, outdance and outsing any competition in sight. It was a quintet distinguished by the breadth and balance of its singing talent, which ran the gamut from David Ruffin's harsh baritone to Eddie Kendricks's wispy falsetto.

The group had been formed in Detroit in the early Sixties, but many members came from the South. Eddie Kendricks had migrated to Detroit from Birmingham, Alabama, in hopes of rebuilding his old group, the Primes, and met Ruffin, a longtime Motor City resident born in Mississippi. The quintet's music reflected its background: of all the Motown acts, the Temptations were the closest to church and gospel roots.

Working primarily with Smokey Robinson and Norman Whitfield, the Temptations enjoyed a number of hits in a variety of styles. At the outset, Kendricks dominated the group, seeing the Tempts through such early R&B hits as "The Way You Do the Things You Do" (Robinson, 1964) and "Girl (Why You Wanna Make Me Blue)" (Whitfield, 1964.) After Robinson's "My Girl" (1965), featuring Ruffin, introduced the group to a white audience, Robinson ran through a sequence of ballads pitting Ruffin's raspy voice against violins, a phase climaxing with Smokey's brilliant "Since I Lost My Baby" (1965). But the Temptations only hit their popular peak under Whitfield's tutelage. Unlike Holland-Dozier-Holland, Whitfield had a flair for spacious rhythmic arrangements. He also had the good sense to exploit the Temptations' versatility, moving from the gritty drive of "(I Know) I'm Losing You" (1966) to "You're My Everything" (1967), a melodramatic wall of sound that featured Ruffin and Kendricks swapping leads.

After Ruffin left the group in 1968, Whitfield turned to more declamatory material; influenced by Sly Stone, he brought the Tempts into the psychedelic era ("Cloud Nine," 1968), and began writing didactic social commentary ("Ball of Confusion," from 1970, for example). All these stratagems, however, could scarcely conceal the fact that Ruffin's departure had upset the group's distinctive balance; while the Temptations remained a potent commercial force, they rarely recaptured the glories of their earlier work. Nevertheless, two singles stand out: "I Can't Get Next to You" (1960), a neoclassical throwback to Whitfield's original style, and "Just My Imagination (Running Away with Me)" (1971), a gossamer showcase for Eddie Kendricks, who went solo shortly afterward.

Supremes. Without a doubt, Diana Ross and the Supremes were Berry Gordy's consummate commercial coup. In the span of five years, they amassed 12 Number One pop hits—five in a row after "Where Did Our Love Go" in 1964. A record unrivaled by any other female group in pop, it attests to the skill with which Holland-Dozier-Holland and Gordy packaged the Supremes and their music.

Discovered by Gordy in Detroit, where the trio had grown up together in the Brewster housing project, the Supremes floundered for almost a year until they were hooked up with Holland-Dozier-Holland in 1963. Their first collaboration, "When the Lovelight Starts Shining Through His Eyes," a torrid, brassy up-tempo track, became a modest pop hit in late 1963.

But H-D-H didn't have quite the right formula for the group down yet. After a followup flopped, they devised a medium-tempo song that accentuated Ross's insouciant delivery: "Where Did Our Love Go," a Number One pop hit in the summer of 1964, set the pattern for the singles that followed. Ross cultivated a nonchalant, almost fey style, while H-D-H turned numerous variations on the theme of lost love. During Holland-Dozier-Holland's tenure with the Supremes, the hits were automatic: between "Where Did Our Love Go" and the end of 1967, the Supremes released 15 singles; with one exception, they all made the Top Ten, and ten of them made Number One.

In a sense, the H-D-H Supremes hits are the purest expression of the Motown sound. The most compliant of Motown's artists, Diana Ross meshed seamlessly with the cyclical structure Holland-Dozier-Holland favored. Her singles resembled one long composition, each new release slightly modifying an element in the overall design, perhaps adding strings or punching the tempo up a notch. By "You Keep Me Hangin' On" (1966), the approach had become so polished that Diana Ross and the Supremes began to sound like an erotic gloss on the assembly-line existence Gordy had adopted in organizing Motown—and in this respect as well, the Supremes were the ultimate embodiment of the Motown ethos.

The key to the Supremes was Ross, who quickly overshadowed her fellow Supremes, visually as well as vocally. Peering with Keane eyes from under a variety of oversized wigs and baroque hairdos, her skinny frame draped in an array of slinky outfits, she was the very picture of the seductive self-pity her lyrics usually articulated ("Nothing but Heartaches"). At the same time, she became a paragon of black respectability; although Gordy found the Supremes "giggly and immature" when he signed them, he soon had reason to be proud of the most illustrious product of his in-house finishing school. By the time Ross left the group in 1969, the Supremes were fixtures on the supper-club circuit. Ross, of course, went on to stardom in the cinema. In 1976, Florence Ballard, one of the other original Supremes, died in Detroit; she had been on and off welfare the last few years.

Gladys Knight and the Pips. Before they came to Motown, Gladys Knight and the Pips were sporadically popular balladeers; after they arrived, Norman Whitfield converted them into consistent hitmakers. On the original "I Heard It through the Grapevine" (1967), Knight was transformed into a fiery hard-edge vocalist, unleashing her scorn with startling fury. But unlike Martha Reeves, Knight was too versatile a singer to be limited to one role; by the early Seventies, the funky persona of Whitfield's productions (such as "The Nitty Gritty," in 1969) had given way to the vulnerable lover of "If I Were Your Woman" (1970). After leaving the label, Knight and the Pips, unlike most Motown alumni, actually consolidated their popularity by reverting to such glossy pop ballads as "Midnight Train to Georgia" (1973).

Jackson 5. "Discovered" by Diana Ross in a Gary, Indiana, club, this quintet of Hoosiers proved to be not only the last great Motown act, but also the last great gasp of Gordy's assembly-line entity. Fronted by the exuberant Michael Jackson, who dipped, spun amd moved like a miniature James Brown, the Jackson 5 transcended all barriers of race and age in their appeal; they even hosted a Saturday morning cartoon show for a spell. Unlike many of their prepubescent imitators, however, the J5's talent was strictly for real. As the group matured, so did their music, but though later tracks like "Get It Together" (1973) and "Forever Came Today" (1975) were innovative, tight productions, the best Jackson 5 record remained their first for Motown, "I Want You Back" (1969). Catalyzed by a red-hot performance from ten-year-old-Michael, the record explodes off the turntable with an intri-

cate Sly-influenced arrangement featuring some of the toughest
bass, drum, piano and guitar playing on any soul record anywhere.

While one facet of the Motown saga is well documented by
the consistent popularity of its central acts, a much hazier part of
the story has been buried beneath the glitter, purposely obscured
to prevent any tarnishing of the corporate image.

To the outside world, Motown seemed like one big happy
family. While a number of Motown stars have confirmed the ac-
curacy of this picture in the early Sixties, by the middle of the decade serious problems had begun to appear. The autocratic
determination that had carried Gordy's company to the top could
not help but foster resentment, especially as Gordy's protégés became used to their status in the limelight.

Yet the company continued to control virtually every relevant
detail of a performer's career, dictating the songs to be sung, the
producers to be used, the singles to be released, the image to be
presented to the public (even Motown's biggest stars remained
curiously nondescript; reliable biographical details were few and
far between). In financial affairs, Gordy governed his flock with
patronizing authority: his younger stars were kept on allowances,
ostensibly to help them avoid the pitfalls that had left other nou-
veau riche R&B stars penniless at 30.

His attitude toward the Supremes was typical. "We had some
trouble with them at first," Gordy said in 1966. "You must be very
strict with young artists. That instills discipline. But once they get
a Number One record, they tend to get more independent. They
start spending their money extravagantly. . . . After a year, they
saw their mistakes and came to appreciate our handling of their
affairs." Though their yearly income was in the five-figures—
record royalties were divided equally—they were on an allow-
ance of $50 a week.

In late 1967, the first major crack appeared in the Motown
facade. Holland-Dozier-Holland demanded an accounting of
their royalties. Shortly after a suit was initiated, the trio left Motown to form their own label and production firm: a move that
neither Motown or H-D-H ever fully recovered from.

But internal dissension was not the only problem plaguing
Gordy. By 1968, the industry had begun to catch up with the Motown sound. Without Holland-Dozier-Holland, neither the Su-

premes nor the Four Tops were able to maintain their popularity. Even worse, the label's new properties were becoming rare; only Gladys Knight and the Jackson 5 were able to match the style and talent of earlier Motown acts. Gordy himself increasingly retreated from company affairs, choosing instead to lavish his attention on Diana Ross, who was being groomed for a career in Hollywood.

In 1971, both Stevie Wonder and Marvin Gaye negotiated contracts giving them artistic control; the same year, the company moved its headquarters from Detroit to Los Angeles. The old studio system was dissolved, and many of the old stars drifted away: by 1975, Martha Reeves, Gladys Knight, the Jackson 5 and the Four Tops had all left. The company's music, with few exceptions, was no longer particularly distinctive; its quality was increasingly erratic. In the unkindest cut of all, Gamble and Huff's Philadelphia combine finally surpassed Motown as the leading purveyors of top-notch assembly-line black pop, using many of the same ingredients that Gordy had parlayed into a corporate empire.

Motown in its heyday, on the other hand, knew no peers. In the end, it was a wholly mechanical style and sound that roared and purred like a well-tuned Porsche. Contrived yet explosive, the very epitome of mass-produced pop yet drenched in the black tradition, the Motown hits of the Sixties revolutionized American popular music. Never again would black performers be confined to the fabled chitlin circuit; never again would black popular music be dismissed as a minority taste. For more than a decade, Berry Gordy and his many talented cohorts managed, with unerring verve and against all the odds, to translate a black idiom into "The Sound of Young America." Aesthetically as well as commercially, Motown's achievement will likely remain unrivaled for years to come.

SOME FUTURE[4]

The erotic authority of Little Richard, the acrobatic dexterity of Chuck Berry, the bemused sexuality of Mick Jagger, the arrogant energy of Bob Dylan, above all the innocent pleasure in mastery shown by Elvis Presley amid the mayhem of his first televised triumphs—all this was made vivid again in the finely picked images that comprised *The Heroes of Rock and Roll*, a special aired on February 8, 1979, by ABC-TV. Yet the parade from past to present aroused mixed feelings. Exhilarated once more by the immediacy of Presley, I was doubly depressed by the dreary professionalism of Fleetwood Mac, the stale showmanship of Elton John, the nervous posturing of Bruce Springsteen. The juxtaposition of these later clips with the earlier ones only threw into relief the calculation and shallowness of most rock in the 1970s. Heading into the last half hour, the host informed us that "as the 1960s came to an end, the optimism of Woodstock began to sour. . . . But what kept rock going in the 1970s was great groups." He should have been more honest. In the 1970s, there are no longer heroes of rock and roll.

This may seem unfair. Yet whatever their musical talents, performers like Fleetwood Mac, Elton John and Linda Ronstadt project either an unsatisfying aura of canned charisma, or no aura at all: in the large arenas where they play, they seem dwarfed, unimpressive. Even Bruce Springsteen acts like a self-conscious imposter, as if he had spent too much time in front of a mirror figuring out how to look heroic. And Elvis Costello, currently the most vital performer in rock, too knowingly plays the sardonic and self-deprecating victim to qualify as a world conqueror. The distance from Presley to Costello is the distance from James Dean to Woody Allen.

In the 1970s, there are only anti-heroes and "platinum acts." When an album sells one million or more copies, it is awarded a platinum disk. People in the record business—an industry that, in the last few years, has become more profitable than either television or movies—seem to think that anything less than a platinum disk is some kind of indecency. In a recent interview in

[4]Excerpted from a magazine article by music columnist Jim Miller. *The New Republic.* 108:25–8. Mr 24, '79.

Rolling Stone, a senior vice-president for sales and promotion at Warner Brothers explained that:

[t]oday, the average cost of producing an album is between $100,000 and $150,000. To send an artist on tour we have to support that tour. We have to bring [press and radio] people into the clubs, pay for their drinks and food. We have to advertise the artist's appearance in the club and the fact that he has a record out. We have to put out posters and other merchandising aids for stores. Unfortunately, sometimes we go out and spend this money and the record doesn't sell.

The idea is to pick sure-fire new acts, break them quickly, get them out of the clubs and into the arenas, and sell as many records as possible, preferably a million or more. Avarice draws its own morals. According to a spokesman for CBS records, "it's not enough to have a hit single to break an album. That only means sales of 300,000 to 500,000 copies. We're looking for platinum, and that requires marketing."

Against the backdrop of this omnipresent and increasingly centralized corporate machinery, some critics have cast about restlessly for a figure who fits their idea of a new hero; someone able to surmount the established routines, someone willing to flout the caution of corporate calculations. Their search for new heroes began early in the 1970s. Candidates have included the New York Dolls, Bruce Springsteen, Graham Parker, the Sex Pistols and Elvis Costello. Some of these failed to command popular attention, a fatal flaw. Others got attention, but only with the help of record company hype, a fault especially damaging when the aspiring hero too obviously lowers his sights to meet standardized expectations.

Of course, it is worth remembering that Elvis Presley arrived in New York City with Colonel Tom Parker, one of the greatest hucksters in the history of show business. But the Colonel, who cut his teeth working concessions for the Great Parker Pony Circus, dreamed of scams scaled to the eccentric ambitions of a self-made impresario. To the end, his idea of marketing was to stand by himself outside of the halls where Presley appeared, selling glossy photos of the idol. Who needed middlemen? Now, hawking heroes can be crass—Presley's career is the proof—but it isn't the same thing as marketing platinum. The difference involves getting the public to believe that the world's best hamburger is made in Tupelo, Mississippi, rather than flooding the country with hamburger franchises.

But the search for new idols continues, and critics aren't the only ones doing the looking. If writers want something to cheer about, record companies have an understandable interest in made-to-order mythology. So the desire for heroes lingers, despite the growing implausibility of the wish: in the 1970s, to want to be a hero is, almost inevitably, to become instead a mere "platinum act," prepackaged, marketed and dwarfed, just like all the rest. Yet to appreciate the lure of this desire, as well as its risks, is to begin to understand why the Sex Pistols and Elvis Costello—and, more generally, "punk" and "new wave"—have had such an impact, however indirectly, on rock in the late 1970s.

Among the diminishing number of my friends who still listen seriously to rock, and certainly among my critical colleagues, there is a virtual consensus that rock and roll in the last couple of years has undergone a major renewal. The annual critics' poll conducted by the *Village Voice* produced the front-page banner headline "Triumph of the New Wave." As if in counterpoint, on February 2, the news came that Sid Vicious, once a member of punk's premier band, the Sex Pistols, had overdosed on heroin, shortly after being released from prison on bail; the previous fall, he had been accused of murdering his girlfriend. The wire service obituary didn't give much evidence of triumph: "When the Sex Pistols finally reached the United States [late in 1977], their tour was a flop. They drew small crowds and bad reviews."

II

What was punk, what is the new wave, and why did serious listeners respond enthusiastically while the wider American audience largely ignored this new music?

If punk died on Friday, February 2, 1979, it was born on Friday, November 6, 1975. That was the day the Sex Pistols played their first concert, at a British art school. Offended by the caterwauling of the band, the social secretary of the school pulled the plug, cutting the concert short after five minutes. Punk begins with a confrontation: its medium is hostility, its aim to shock.

In Britain, punk became a battle cry, a rallying point, an expression of resentments rooted in class differences. A drop-out at 16 and briefly a janitor, Johnny Rotten, self-professed antichrist and lead singer of the Sex Pistols, almost singlehandedly invented punk as an incendiary happening. The Sex Pistols blew the boards clean; into the space they cleared stepped others, most notably the Clash. In New York City, the movement found antecedents in the New York Dolls, allies in hard rockers like the Ramones, and fellow-travelers in avant-gardists like Television, Talking Heads and Patti Smith. But where the New Yorkers were older, cooler and artier, the British punks were young, angry and hell-bent on fame, assaulting the pop scene head on, polarizing listeners and prompting righteous warnings about renewed teen barbarism. What in America remained an artifact of cult interest, in Great Britain quickly became a cultural battleground. English leftists hotly debated the revolutionary merits and neo-fascist vices of this violent music, while American record executives converged on London to see whether punk could be profitably exported.

If, in context, punk was a gesture of defiance that defined a style of life, out of context and simply staring at lyrics, its point seems deceptively clear.

> When there's no future
> How can there be sin
> We're the flowers in the dustbin
> We're the poison in your human machine
> We're the future
> Your future
> God save the Queen
> We mean it man
> There is no future
> No future for you
> No future for me.

Those are the words Johnny Rotten sings on "God Save the Queen," one of the few transcendent moments of rock and roll in this decade. Yet listening to the record, it's virtually impossible to tell what the lyrics are, and it doesn't even matter, because the whole exhilarating, shattering, nihilistic message is condensed in the brute fact of the music's unforgiving presence.

In the great anthems of British punk—"God Save the Queen," "Anarchy in the U.K." by the Sex Pistols, "White Riot" by the Clash—the lyrics are spit up from a roiling mass of guitars, globs of venom from the bowels of a viper. Intentionally abrasive, the sonorities sabotage any glib response. Beside the immediacy of the sound, the lyrics are mere accessories. The gale of noise is so harsh that these records often produce an overwhelming sense of claustrophobia in unprepared listeners. "God Save the Queen" and "White Riot" are not records that accommodate indifference. To surrender to their raw power, though, is to find serenity amid the tumult: listening to punk is not without its moments of catharsis.

If punk guitarists hurl aural barbs, while the bassists thump spasmodically and the drummers limn the meters of disorder, the vocalists either squall or mince. Some follow Johnny Rotten, who commands an arsenal of primal screams, an unrelenting mode of expression that begins where Little Richard once climaxed. Others follow David Byrne, lead singer for the Talking Heads, who affects an eviscerated singsong more evocative of an idling robot than an uncontrollable antichrist.

Whatever path its vocalists take, punk is vehement, a music of measured virulence. It arose at a time when rock had become "good music" played by platinum acts. It revolted against musical expertise as well as the corporate machinery of pop. In doing so, punk radically reaffirmed rock's democratic promise: in Sly Stone's phrase, "everybody is a star." Yet for the punks the promise was simultaneously a threat—of the unstoppable return of the repressed, an angry mob of mutants' converging on Metropolis. The sock hop of the 1950s and the love-in of the 1960s were replaced by dress balls for discards, a community of demonstrative outcasts to complement the show on stage. In a setting which blurred the line between spectators and performers, flashy freakiness assumed an erotic significance, while the ritual display of destructiveness evoked a perverse heroism: the charisma of the social casualty. Within this community, the exchange of abuse offered proof of solidarity.

By design, punk is not easy. One of the Clash's British singles has a symptomatic label indebted to Roy Lichtenstein: it depicts a smoking comic-strip pistol aimed directly at the viewer. By its sheer volume and cheerful violence, this agit-prop pop relentlessly pummels its audience. It is meant to force involvement. When punk works, it bypasses thinking judgment to tap a more visceral vein. And that, paradoxically, makes punk peculiarly demanding, an artifact that cannot be held at bay through cerebral detachment, a "popular music" that averts almost all the pop formulas for entertainment. Even the essential rock clichés about fun are blown apart with a gruesome irony that makes hedonism sound like a pretty bad bet. Pauline Kael has recently noticed among

"more discriminating" moviegoers a fear of films that too graphi-
cally depict violence. We could just as well talk about a fear of
punk.

But what has killed punk is not only its difficulty, or even its
self-inflicted wounds. From the outset, it struck a stance en-
meshed in contradictions. To the extent they became big stars,
the Sex Pistols and the Clash inevitably compromised the radicalism of punk's democratic promise. For a movement that claimed
to flout the canons of corporate commercialism, the competition
for contracts with big record companies proved peculiarly keen.
Independent labels showed unusual resourcefulness in enhancing
the exchange value of their commodity: limited pressings, colored vinyl, and a variety of picture sleeves made punk records instantly collectible. Even worse, the use of rock to shock quickly
became predictable, and hence not very shocking. In punk as in
dada, *épater le bourgeoisie* works only once; by the second time, cynicism sets in.

These contradictions define the limits of punk. Faced with
them, Joe Strummer, lead singer and lyricist for the Clash, tries
bravely to sound hopeful. "We've got loads of contradictions for
you," he recently boasted to an interviewer. "We're trying to do
something new; we're trying to be the greatest group in the
world, and that also means the biggest. At the same time, we're
trying to be radical—I mean, we never want to be *really* respectable—and maybe the two can't coexist, but we'll try." Yet perhaps the most serious contradiction isn't even the one between
ambition and rebellion: in rock and roll, that's a story that starts
with Elvis Presley.

Far deadlier is punk's atavism. Since refinement and style are
perceived as props for social control, punk's showy musical Jud-
dism entails a stubbornly static form of rock conservatism. The
anti-art conventions of punk become an obligatory code even
more constricting than those initially rejected. Yet despite its
proud display of primitivism, punk is peculiarly "arty." In the spirit of self-conscious minimalism, it makes a statement that solicits
interpretation rather than merely providing a thoughtless diversion. But since artistry per se is suspect, the conventions of punk
don't invite bold departures or virtuoso self-expression. The mu-
sicianly ingenuity of Elvis Costello—the surprising harmonic
modulations in his songs, the audacious intervals in his melodic
lines—disqualifies him as a punk. To quote *Sluggo*, a punk fanzine

published in Austin, Texas, Costello's new album "Sucks. Out loud. Elvis Costello tastes Mass Acceptance. He wants it, maybe he'll get it. He can go to hell."

It is no surprise that a little punk goes a long way. Once past the great recorded landmarks—a handful of singles by the Sex Pistols, the Clash and a few others, like the original versions of Magazine's "Shot by Both Sides" and Devo's "Jocko Homo"—punk is notable primarily for its high-energy trashiness. At its brightest, with bands like Wire and the Ramones, it's a kick. At its bleakest, with a band like Pere Ubu, it is disarming and disturbing—a mirror held up to postindustrial decay. But on the average, punk is mainly monotonous. Stripped out of context and reduced to the minimal conventions communicable on a recording, most of it is about as challenging as Star Trek reruns.

On the other hand, punk's contradictions are only those of rock writ large. Faced with the appalling post-hippie *Zeitgeist* expressed by singers like Joni Mitchell and Jackson Browne—"survivors" all too eager to let us know they've decided to grow up—punk restored a cutting edge to pop without indulging in the sodden pyrotechnics and tedious swagger of Led Zeppelin and Bad Company. It has reminded a new audience that rock and roll is about chancy fun as much as carefree escape, and it has restored some meaning and feeling to a music gone flat.

In its passion, politics and will to power, punk belongs to the mainstream of rock and roll. In the dead ends into which it has obstinately driven, it merely exposes the predicaments of rock in the 1970s. At a time and in a field in which the opportunities for uncontrived heroism seem all but foreclosed, punk staked its claim to authenticity through self-immolation. Its conceit was its glory, its triumph a form of suicide—all things considered, a tough act to follow.

BACK ON THE STREET AGAIN[5]

If you were looking for an image to hold on to—and who isn't these days?—you couldn't have found a more encouraging one. It was St. Patrick's Day in Boston, and a crush of about 1,200 whites and blacks, gays and straights, had come together to see a black 20-year old pop genius named Prince unite rock and roll's exhibitionism with R&B's sexual wit. For his encore Prince wore only a shiny black bikini and a red bandanna. He floated a feather-light ballad on the wings of his falsetto, which he followed with a guitar solo that kicked, whinnied and reared before galloping off in the distance. Smokey Robinson and Jimi Hendrix. Romance and pornography. Dion and Johnny Rotten. Innocence and fury. Prince swung among all of them, and for an hour and a half this late-20th-century dance seemed not only graceful and heroic, but necessary. At a time when white audiences and black audiences—the pop charts and the pop underground—have almost nothing to do with one another, Prince is insisting that they do.

He's about the only one. Last March, if you had turned on Top 40 radio—the one place where white and black music have always been free to jostle each other—you would have heard only four songs by black performers. By the fall the figure had increased slightly to seven songs. You have to go back 25 years—to the pre-rock-and-roll era—to find so little black music topping the pop charts. While it would be easy to blame Reagan, corporate mendacity and the Mandrell Sisters for this situation, it would not be very useful. There are other, more complex explanations, and they mount up like small change.

• The collapse of disco as mass culture. Disco, as several critics have noted, was the music of the affirmative action generation. It encouraged gays, straights, blacks, whites, Europeans and Americans to mix it up on the dance floor and in the studio. It was also one of the few types of black music that could mobilize and exploit pop's huge mainstream audience. When, in 1979, disco fragmented into a collection of devotees' cults, many blacks acts were without a marketplace and identity.

[5]Reprint of a magazine article by Kit Rachlis, executive editor of the *Village Voice. Mother Jones.* 7:12+. Ja. '82. Copyright © 1982 by *Mother Jones.*

• The collapse of Top 40 radio. By the mid-'70s, the most effective way to market pop records was to gain airplay on FM stations, which play album cuts instead of singles. While this was once the sign of a freer format, most FM stations now—for all their liberal patina and hip parlance—follow play lists that are far more white than the old rah-rah AM stations.

• The conservatization of mainstream pop culture. First anticipating and then confirming Reagan's victory, an increasing number of country and western songs have "crossed over" to become pop hits. It would be a mistake to assume that all the recent country-oriented songs in the Top 40 have been pablum (not when you include Dolly Parton's cheerfully subversive "9 to 5"), but most of the C&W pop hits have been—to borrow a Texasism—all hat and no saddle. Needless to say, C&W is white.

• The liberalization of mainstream pop culture. New Wave is now the sound of young America. A glorification of anybody-can-do-it amateurism, New Wave was a dismissal of anything that smacked of the professional, the smooth, the produced, the virtuosic. What most people had in mind was Mick Jagger, Bad Company, the Eagles—rock's corporate elite—but this sweeping rejection also included black pop, a genre that could never afford to cultivate incompetence the way that a band like the New York Dolls could. For all its subversiveness, New Wave is the first type of rock to draw almost nothing from American black music.

• The blanding out of black pop. Without disco and without a dominant sound (like Philly soul) or a dominant company (like Motown) to give it a center, black pop in 1981 was incapable of galvanizing the mainstream audience. There were exceptions—Smokey Robinson's "Being With You," the Pointer Sisters' "Slow Hand," Deniece Williams' "Silly"—but if little black music crossed over to the pop charts in the past few years, it was because little of it demanded attention.

One of pop music's lasting pleasures is that though everything is supposed to be on the surface—it's a music that places emphasis on energy and image, right?—few things are what they seem. So while black music was being shut out of the Top 40 in 1980—shut out from the possibility of having a wide audience—it was undergoing a rebellion that was as significant as the British punk explosion in 1977. And like most pop rebellions, this one took its limitations—shaky finances, tiny audiences, narrow style—and transformed them into advantages. This rebellion doesn't have an adequate name: "new street music" comes closest. But even that name doesn't convey the openness of a scene that, early on, accepted a British singer like Kelly Marie ("Feels Like I'm in Love") and the African/Canadian duo responsible for putting together Lime ("Your Love"). Like punk, the new street music was bonded more by what it rejected than what it projected. And the 12-inch singles, which began coming out of New York City in late 1980, ignored all the rules of marketing, polish and decorum that had grown up in the boom years of the '70s. In short, they ignored all that was slick and big-time about black pop.

These singles were rough, zealous, insistent. They were issued on tiny labels like Enjoy, Sugarhill, Dazz and Etcetera. Some were one-person operations thrown up just to produce the record; all, at first, relied on New York's informal network of DJs, fans, clubs and specialty record stores for distribution. This was music made in and for the city. Sometimes you got the feeling that the musicians were singing only for their neighborhood and social circle, which somehow had jammed into the studio to join them. What you hear on these records is what you hear on all great rock and R&B records—the sound of remaking the world and claiming your place in it.

By St. Patrick's Day 1981, it was possible to dip blindly into a singles bin and come out with a half-dozen different but equally exciting records, including Taana Gardner's slower-than-slow, agonizing modern-day blues, "Heartbeat"; Chaud's transformation of the Grass Roots hit "Midnight Confessions" into a gay anthem; Wanda "Star" Williams' witty, knowing, mid-afternoon fantasy, "Soap Opera Lover"; Debra Dejean's cool 'n' trashy, I-can-out-Deborah-Harry-anytime, "Goosebumps"; Lime's electronically jazzed-up soul ballad "Your Love." And then there were the rappers, who swarmed over and under everything, whose very names gave away their aspirations, their cockiness, their theater: Grandmaster Flash and the Furious Five, Count Coolout, Kurtis Blow, the Treacherous Three, Funky Four + 1.

Rap is at the center of the new street music, because it is most obviously a scavenger's art—making do with what you find or what you steal. Simply described, rap consists of rhymed lines, more spoken than sung, over a rhythm track that is often "borrowed" from other songs. The lines usually have internal rhymes as well and follow an up-and-down or a hippity-hop beat. With its roots in kids' games like "the dozens," Muhammad Ali's prefight poems and the practice of DJs talking over records, rap is essentially a long boast—the aural equivalent of graffiti. In critic Mike Freedberg's words, they are advertisements of the self, but they are extraordinarily generous, communal advertisements. Almost all the best raps—Grandmaster Flash's "Freedom" and Funky Four's "That's the Joint"—are performed by groups, and most incorporate shouts and responses from friends and fans.

For rock critics, the similarities between rap and punk seemed overwhelming. Once again, the music was being carried by singles, not albums; singles were immediate, newsy and (most important) cheap, while albums were expensive and slow in the making. Once again, the music was being made by independent labels, primitive capitalists who were far more nimble and responsive than the big corporations. And, once again, the music put a premium on feeling rather than technical skill; the new street music was accessible, keeping pop's democratic promise that anyone can do it.

But the punk parallel falls down in some crucial ways. Unlike rock, where semipopularity has long been accepted, R&B has had no choice but to be upwardly mobile. To have a No. 1 hit is a performer's highest achievement in the genre. Grandmaster Flash and Funky Four + 1 and their record companies, Sugarhill and Enjoy, are no doubt pleased that money can be made when a single sells only 40,000 copies, but, make no mistake, what they're looking for is hits. Then, not only have they transformed their neighborhood into the world, but they have also transformed the world into their neighborhood.

Black music traditionally has absorbed its rebellions much faster than rock and roll. It took commercial rock two years to respond to punk, but by the fall of 1981, the new street music was shaping the R&B charts. Not only that—the new street music had crossed over and had provided the pop charts with two of its biggest and best summer hits: "Double Dutch Bus," by Frankie Smith; and "Square Biz," by Teena Marie. It is a measure of how much the new music opened everything up, because these hits were form the least likely sources. Frankie Smith is a mid-30-ish professional songwriter, laid off by Philly International during the industry-wide recession two years ago. Teena Marie is a white soul singer on Motown whose audience is almost exclusively black.

Their two hits, as much as anything, sum up what is best about street music. *Double dutch* and *square biz* are slang—private code words. Smith uses *double dutch*, taken from rope-skipping exercise, to describe the rhythm of walking through city streets; Teena Marie uses *square biz* to mean the truth. Listening to both songs, you hear an irrepressibility, a refusal to be ignored. Smith missed his bus to work, so he marches on. Teena is not going to let Blondie overshadow her. But mostly what you hear on these records—and it's what you hear on all the street records—is the joy of coming out of nowhere and making everyone look up and take notice.

SONGS FROM THE HIGH GROUND[6]

Songs for the starving of the world. Concerts to bolster the struggling small farms of America. *Do They Know It's Christmas?* and *We Are the World.* Band Aid and Live Aid.

Feel as if the collective spirit of rock has suddenly been hot-wired for social activism? Fine. Think this will blow over in a little, and everything will settle down? Think again; that is not going to happen for a while. There are two immediate reasons why: the release the week of Oct. 14 of an impassioned all-star antiapartheid record, *Sun City,* and the congenial reverberations from last week's FarmAid, the concert that featured top rock and country-and-western talent drumming up support for the American farmer. Both the *Sun City* record and the FarmAid concert, held at a football stadium in Champaign, Ill., celebrate a unity within the music community even as they signal a further deepening of social awareness.

That works in both political directions. Neil Young stumped heavily at the concert for the controversial Harkin bill, which is also known as the "Farm Policy Reform Act of 1985," while the Charlie Daniels Band held down the conservative wing with banner-waving ditties like *In America,* which offered the observation that Lady Liberty "may have stumbled, but she ain't never fell."

[6]Reprint of a magazine article by staff writer Jay Cocks and staff reporters. *Time.* 126:78+. O. 7, '85. Copyright © 1985 Time Inc. All rights reserved. Reprinted by permission from *TIME.*

Lou Reed pointed up the irony of rock, freshly politicized, being attacked for excessive raunch, by recalling "those people who are trying to censor records" before launching into his classic *Walk on the Wild Side.*

Live Aid may have been slicker and more elaborate, but Farm Aid had the edge musically. There were frequent appearances throughout the 14 ¼-hour event by Co-Organizer Willie Nelson, whose heavy responsibilities never weighted the sensual ease of his vocals. There were also high-spirited performances by Co-Organizer John Cougar Mellencamp, Bonnie Raitt, Loretta Lynn and Emmylou Harris, and an incendiary set by Bob Dylan, whose remarks at Live Aid about American farm troubles, says Nelson, "put the idea [for FarmAid] in my head." Perhaps the fleetest combination of hard music and solid sentiment came during John Fogerty's appearance, his first before a paying audience since 1972. After playing two songs from his new album, and before launching into a drop-dead version of the R.-and-B. classic *Knock on Wood,* Fogerty simply reminded the enthusiastic audience of 78,000, "The next time you sit down to a very nice meal, remember, it didn't come from a cellophane bag from Safeway. Some guy gave his whole life to that meal you're eating."

Sun City will add a fresher and far angrier voice to this chorus of conscience. Its heat, its rhythm and its political passion, in fact, set it apart from the congenial charity of other all-star predecessors. *Sun City* may be one of the year's best singles. Certainly it is the boldest.

The song is aimed at a broad musical spectrum, from rock to rap, and has the kind of forceful beat and dense layering that can pulverize the floor of a dance club at 3 o'clock in the morning. "That's the first level of communication," says Steve Van Zandt, who, as Little Steven, wrote the song and coproduced it with Arthur Baker. "Everybody likes to dance." If everybody can hold still long enough and listen to some lyrics, however, he will get an earful. *Sun City* is aimed right at the top of the charts, but its sentiments are not the sort of material usually found in *Billboard*'s "Hot 100."

As Artists United Against Apartheid, as many as 49 performers sing on *Sun City,* whose title evokes a Vegas-style entertainment complex stuck improbably in a South African "homeland." Jazz (Miles Davis) is on the record. So is folk (Jackson Browne, Raitt), Latin (Rubén Blades) and reggae (Jimmy Cliff), along with

the royalty of rock, both domestic (Daryl Hall) and imported
(Pete Townshend, Ringo Starr). Van Zandt's original concept for
a single and a dance remix has become a mini-LP of material.
Among the tracks: a coruscating jazz version of *Sun City* by Davis,
Keyboardist Herbie Hancock, Bass Player Ron Carter and Drummer Tony Williams; a free-flowing political, rhythmic stream of
consciousness by Ray Barretto, Peter Wolf, Rapper Grandmaster
Melle Mel and Soweto's Malopoets; and a meditation by Progressive Rock Wizard Peter Gabriel.

It is the single, however, that will probably attract the most
attention and provoke the greatest response. If, as Rock Critic
Greil Marcus has skeptically suggested, the recent spate of concerts like FarmAid bespeaks merely "a craze for charity," then
Sun City represents a step toward outright activism. The accustomed structure for all such undertakings is present: participat-
ing musicians worked free, recording studios donated facilities,
Van Zandt covered his own expenses, and Manhattan Records
will donate all of the profits to the nonprofit Africa Fund.

What is new, however, is the sound of some of the world's best
musicians putting it straight on the line. David Ruffin of the
Temptations and Browne sing about "relocation to phony
homelands." Cliff and Hall remember "people are dying and giving up hope," and Darlene Love jumps in with "This quiet diplo-
macy ain't nothing but a joke." The clincher comes with the hard
challenge of Bruce Springsteen's voice, which should be some
strong indication of rock's new course. Anyone ever hear Elvis
Presley sing a song about Martin Luther King Jr.? On *Sun City*,
the country's most formidable rocker since Presley's passing can
be heard making his feelings quite clear: "We're stabbing our
brothers and sisters in the back."

"Message songs," says Hancock, "get a little boring. You begin
to sound like missionaries. With *Sun City*, though, you get caught
in the rhythms." The rhythms are new, but in fact this vocal conscience comes out of a long tradition. There were activist antecedents in the alternative culture of the '60s, but those were self-
absorbed and, as both Browne and Van Zandt point out, were
intermingled with the drug culture. Perhaps inspired by such
punk guerrilla bands as Britain's Clash and the Sex Pistols in the
late '70s, rock has buried higher consciousness under high conscience. "It's a rebirth of the spirit we had in the '60s, but it is a

little more pragmatic," says Don Henley, whose performance of his *A Month of Sundays* at FarmAid was a high point.

Joan Baez, who agrees that this all represents "some kind of phenomenon," also suggests, "Rock 'n' rollers are answering a need of young people to make something out of ashes and silence. They have no leadership, no hero. They've been left nothing. But it's not just the kids. People in my generation or a little younger are longing for something they tasted and that went away." Comments Van Zandt: "The trend of activism is a natural thing after ten to 15 years of being in a coma."

The traces of public drowsiness can still be found. FarmAid seems to have fallen short on phone-in donations. The total just after the concert was only between $8 million and $10 million, although subsequent contributions, as well as the sale of records and videos, may kick that amount higher. Nelson professed to be well pleased. What's important, he told *Time* Correspondent Lee Griggs, "is not the money so much as making people aware of the problem. That FarmAid phone number's going to be there for a year so people can contribute, and we're not gonna let them forget it."

FarmAid will have a lot of healthy competition for attention. Ken Kragen, one of the pivotal organizers of USA for Africa, has no immediate plans for fund-raising concerts but promises other "activities" for next year, observing, "We are in this for the long haul." Bob Geldof, whose Band Aid projects first brought everything to a boil, has helped organize a School Aid program, in which children all over Britain are collecting food for famine relief. He is also on a committee for Fashion Aid, a high-profile show at London's Royal Albert Hall, scheduled for Nov. 5 and featuring the work of such world-class designers as Issey Miyake, Giorgio Armani, Katharine Hamnett and Yves Saint Laurent.

For the moment, however, it is likely to be *Sun City* that sets the beat, quickens the pulse and takes the point for all this musical activism. "Freedom is a privilege, nobody rides for free," is the way Blades and John Oates sing it on the record. The concentrated force of that declaration is a galvanizing message to hear. And there is always this bonus: you can dance to it too.

III. THE ROCK MUSIC INDUSTRY

EDITOR'S INTRODUCTION

There have always been purists who object to the contamination of rock music by big business—especially in the 60s, when there were some who really thought that the demise of capitalism in America was just around the corner. "The bitterest irony is that the 'rock revolution' hype has come close to fatally limiting the revolutionary potential that rock does contain," wrote Michael Lydon in 1969. "If the companies, as representatives of corporate structure, can convince the rock world that their revolution is won or almost won . . . not only will the constituents of rock seal their fate by that fatal self-deception, but their music, one of the few things they actually do have going for them, will have been successfully and truly emasculated." In the 80s, when making money is widely considered the highest form of civilization, big businessmen and rock-and-rollers are exploiting each other with brio, as Drew Moseley points out in her feature from *Rock Yearbook* 1983 on the Rolling Stones, "Jogging for Jovan."

For most of its history, rock music has been dominated by radio, whose programmers decide what gets heard and what doesn't. "Democratic Radio" by Ken Barnes, reprinted from *The First Rock and Roll Confidential Report*, examines in detail the radio formats—Contemporary Hit Radio (Top 40), Album-Oriented ("progressive") Radio, Adult Contemporary—that compete for the market and the advertisers. Since 1981 radio has had to contend with a new rival, the music video, and especially with MTV, a cable television network that airs videos night and day. An article from *Rolling Stone*, "Ad Nauseam: How MTV Sells Out Rock & Roll," by Steven Levy, is a critical look at MTV's emergence as the most influential force in the rock industry, a medium in which the art form and the commercials are indistinguishable— the ultimate marriage of rock music and big business.

In addition to its reluctance to showcase black performers, MTV has been accused of showing videos that overemphasize violence, especially against women, and pornographic sex. Sex, violence, and drugs have been standard rock and roll themes all along, of course, and there have been periodic attempts to censor lyrics and record covers, which are recounted by Steven Dougherty in his *People Weekly* article "From 'Race Music' to Heavy Metal: A Fiery History of Protests." But as Terence Moran recently pointed out in the *New Republic*, "Sex sells in America, and as the advertising world has grown ever more risque in pushing cars, cosmetics, jeans, and liquor to adults, pop music has been forced further past the fringes of respectability for its rebellious thrills. . . . Today's salacious lyrics are not the exception to otherwise generally respected sexual standards and community values, but a symbol of their collapse."

Freedom from restrictions, enjoyment of emotional and physical excess, are the fundamental impulses of rock music, and people who grow up under its spell inevitably must decide how much of that impulse they can continue to follow, at the sacrifice of a more ordered and productive but tamer way of life. Rock stars, who have the opportunity and income to indulge themselves, are notorious for dying young. The final selection, "The Punk Meets the Godmother," is an autobiographical article from *Rolling Stone* by Pete Townshend, a rock star with a gift for seeing rock and roll as a form of spiritual illumination.

JOGGING FOR JOVAN[1]

"Everybody assumes we keep playing for money. But we didn't start this thing for bread and we're not continuing for bread."

Keith Richards

As anyone in the record industry will tell you, tours lose money. It's the nature of the beast, these days, because the astronomical costs of gasoline, sound and lighting alone prohibit profit on the road. No-one goes out with elaborate stage sets any more. Few make enough on record sales to support their tours. Bruce Springsteen, who has never had any trouble selling out his performances, staged a European tour last year that reportedly absorbed costs of nearly a million dollars.

---

[1]Reprint of "Jogging for Jovan," an article by journalist Drew Moseley. In Al Clark, ed., *Rock Yearbook 1983*. St. Martin's Press. '83. Copyright © 1983, St. Martin's Press, New York.

From facts compiled by *Billboard*, of the top ten box-office draws for a week in June 1979 (just before the gas crisis struck), the average attendance for shows in arenas (6,000 to 20,000 seats) was 16,968. For the same period in 1981, the average crowd size was only 10,739—a drop of almost 40 per cent.

Polygram Records' East Coast Director of A&R, Peter Lubin, remarked, "It's one thing to have your band show up in Cleveland. It's another thing if Cleveland doesn't show up."

Promoters have had to withstand escalating costs in all areas—hall rentals, minimum guarantees for bands, stage hand wages, equipment rentals—and they've had to withstand it against the dwindling supply of concert-goers. Either fans can't afford the gas, or they can't afford the ticket prices, or as someone suggested, they've finally come to the conclusion that they can have just as good a time at home, in their rooms, listening to music on their stereos.

This is the situation The Rolling Stones confronted, or ignored, when they set about making plans for an American tour in the summer of 1981. It never occurred to them that they might have to play at a loss, but it seems unlikely that they were fully aware of just how well they could do. "These rumours that the tour will gross $39 million are very exaggerated," a spokeswoman for the band told the press in June of 1981. "They'll be lucky to gross $13 million." . . . As it turned out, the first 13 dates alone grossed more than $15 million in ticket sales, making the $39 million appear, if anything, low. Although the released figures for the gross at the end of the tour state that the amount made was approximately $40 million, if you take into account what was made in the merchandising of Stones T-shirts (at an average of $10.00 a piece) and other artifacts, the figure is probably a great deal higher.

Jagger's business acumen is generally pointed to in reference to the stunning success of the US tour, but he shrugs it off. "I did the budget for this tour in June 1981," he says. "I just looked at it and increased it by 15 per cent. It's not a lot of work." Of course, it helps if you can afford to just look at a tour budget and increase it by 15 per cent. That's one of the advantages of being The Rolling Stones.

It also helps if you can come up with a corporate marriage before the tour begins. The strange courting ritual between corporations and rock 'n' roll has been gaining momentum all through the Seventies, and by the time The Stones were ready to plan their tour, Jovan seemed like the perfect mate. Expert Jay Coleman, whose company Rockbill, Inc. presides over 90 per cent of these corporate/rock 'n' roll mergers, claims that music has become an ideal corporate tie-in. The bands get virtually free money and the corporation gets an inside track to the hearts and minds of the juiciest market of all: adolescents and young adults with taste buds to be formed and money to spend. Jovan reportedly poured $2 million into The Stones tour, in return for which they were allowed to splash the name of their men's cologne all over the concert tickets and radio promotion spots for the tour. While the jury is still out, it's probably the best $2 million they ever spent.

In the Sixties, such a merger would never have been possible, and certainly not with The Stones. Big corporations, the music told us, were part of the problem. Big corporations were responsible for war; they *were* the establishment. But now that The Stones are getting older they could almost pass for establishment too.

"We've never done any of this crap before," said Keith Richards in reference to the Jovan merger. "But we can use the money constructively to pay for small gigs that otherwise we wouldn't have been able to do. It's like a happy medium: Jovan is getting what they want out of it and we're getting some cash up front to pay for gigs that we're going to have to work at a loss . . . with the crew and equipment we've got, by the time they've got the stuff in the front door of those small places, it's costing The Stones bread, you know? *That's* no way to run a tour."

Rehearsals for the mega-tour took place last summer at the Long View Farm in North Brookfield, Massachusetts. The pastoral setting in New England's beautiful woodlands has been a factor in the farm's success since its opening, and bands like J. Geils have recorded some of their most successful LPs there. But The Stones' rehearsals signalled the first encounter for many of the inhabitants of the town with hardcore rock royalty. Armed guards patrolled the compound. Kids snuck close to the buildings in the dead of night for a listen to The Stones.

Rehearsals were generally conducted at night, and some members of the band slept all day and rose at 7pm for the midnight jams. A $40,000 sound stage was designed specifically for the band out of polished pine, with a width of 100 feet, in the main loft.

Jagger, however, did not sleep the day away. His daily regimen included jogging and weight-lifting. "I start working out six months before we go on the road," he explained. "I have to. I run ten miles on stage during every show, and if I don't jog my legs won't last out. But with the weights, the gymnastics and all the other things, there are times when I'm aching so much I can hardly stand up.

"I have to be realistic about it. Physically, I can't go on doing this kind of stage act forever. I feel pretty fit at the moment, but I'll have to change things some day."

The Stones opted to do their first concert incognito at Sir Morgan's Cove, a Worcester, Massachusetts nightclub. They were promoted as "Blue Monday and The Cockroaches" by radio station WAAF, who also distributed the tickets, but rival station WBCN let the cat out of the bag and in addition to the 300 ticket holders, 1,500 fans showed up before midnight. Seventy police officers, some in riot gear, also made an appearance in an effort to keep the peace. But all press was specifically excluded from the show. It was just another rehearsal, Keith later explained. The Stones were using it to determine which songs worked, which didn't, and which might work with a little more practice.

Anyone who saw more than one Stones show, including their first at Philadelphia's JFK Stadium, was quick to point out that the band "didn't really have it together." The sound was awful, the playing wasn't tight, and it was still the most amazing rock performance in recent memory.

The portable stage designed by Kazuhide Yamazaki (who also designed the album cover for *Still Life*, the live album from the US tour) is the largest mobile concert stage ever built, with a 64-foot width, 80-foot ramps stretching out from the right and left sides and another 150 feet of fluttering silk streaming out into the bleachers. The massive scrims surrounding the stage were painted with post-modernist renderings of LPs, guitars and cars and was constructed with 10,000 square feet of cloth. From a 240-foot cherry picker (which also made appearances at most of the other stops on the tour), Jagger dropped armloads of red and white carnations over adoring fans during 'Jumping Jack Flash'.

Bill Wyman, who keeps a record of all The Stones doings since the very beginning on two computers, brought one computer along on the tour with him. According to Wyman, the band finds this " . . . amusing. But every gig we went to on the tour,

Mick would come up to me about ten minutes before we went on to ask when we last played there and in what location. Then we'd go on stage and he'd say, 'Hi, we haven't seen you since 1972, when we played at so-and-so.'"

The band hired an independent auditing firm (to the tune of $500,000) to help with the distribution of tickets. The auditors determined how many potential Stones fans inhabited each zip code area and tickets were allocated accordingly. However, the five west coast shows (one in San Diego and two each in Los Angeles and San Francisco) could accommodate only 100,000, and more than four million pieces of mail were received within 56 hours of the announcement of the concerts. The US Postal Service had to hire 125 part-time employees to deal with the excess.

The Stones had 68 people in their entourage for the outdoor gigs and 52 for the theatres and arenas. In Philadelphia, they had to take over 34 rooms on three floors of the Barclay Hotel, and similar conditions seemed appropriate at their other stops. "They're actually letting us have really nice rooms because we didn't smash them up last tour," Wyman chortled.

The band also hired Ian (Small Faces) MacLagan and Ian Stewart to handle the keyboards for this tour, and there were the usual guest appearances that varied from city to city. They got court orders prohibiting the sale of unauthorized Stones products. They bore the cost of carting their enormous stage and their equally enormous entourage everywhere they went.

As Bill Wyman pointed out, "You don't take the gross and divide it by five. If you divided it by 500, you might be nearer." And promoter Bill Graham will reportedly take 40 per cent of the gross.

Odd as it may sound, it appears that The Stones made some sort of effort to keep expenses reasonable. Their Boulder contract catering rider only specified that American cheese, bologna and dry French red wine be backstage waiting for them after the show.

"You can't spend your life being paranoid. On stage, you can watch the first 30 rows for the nutter with a handgun. But if somebody's out there with a high powered rifle, there's not much you can do about it."

Mick Jagger

Violence still seems to haunt The Stones, although this tour didn't suffer quite the microscopic scrutiny for "bad vibes" it might have considering the lingering reputation that has followed them all the way from Altamont. At the second Seattle, Washington concert on October 15, a woman was arrested when a security guard overheard her threatening Jagger. She was later released and no charges were filed. At the same concert, a 16-year-old girl died of massive head and back injuries after falling 50 feet from an outside stadium ramp onto the Seattle Kingdome parking lot. At the Syracuse, New York concert at the Carrier Dome, nine fans were hospitalized, eight for drunkenness and one girl for a serious cut suffered when she fell over a seat. Another fan was stabbed to death at the Houston performance. A fight between police and fans at the Hartford, Connecticut concert ended in 56 arrests. And a man and a woman, apparently desperate to see The Rolling Stones concert at the Capitol Centre in Landover, Maryland, shot two young men, one fatally, only to learn that the victims didn't have tickets to the event after all.

Mick himself was nearly killed on his way to perform in Syracuse for 43,000 fans. The sheriff's car assigned to take him to the concert was hit broadside by a sports car running a red light. It was pure luck that no-one was seriously hurt.

In Buffalo, the second stop on the tour, 40 knot winds destroyed the original stage set, necessitating the erection of a duplicate, and Jagger's microphone kept smacking him in the mouth. A stop was made before the concert in Rockford, Illinois, so that Jagger could visit a dentist and repair the loosened diamond in his right incisor.

Still, all things considered, the tour was a big success. Small clubs thrived whenever The Stones were in town and had a night off, because rumours ran rampant that The Stones might play. *Tattoo You* had sold in excess of three million copies last January, and the numbers climb still. *Still Life*, featuring songs like "Twenty Flight Rock" and "Goin' To A Go Go," is the long awaited live album from the US tour, and it's expected to do equally well. Especially since it will also serve as the soundtrack for the movie version of the concert, produced by Ron (*Ordinary People*) Schwary and directed by Hal (*Shampoo, Coming Home, Harold and Maude*) Ashby, with cinematographers Caleb Deschanel and Gerry Feil.

Of course, Mick Taylor, The Stones' former lead guitarist, *is* asking the band for big royalties on *Tattoo You* because a couple of tracks (including the hit "Start Me Up," according to one source) are out-takes from the *Goat's Head Soup* LP, which Taylor played on in 1973. But that's just one more minor aggravation. When you're the richest rock and roll band in the world, these things just pop up.

DEMOCRATIC RADIO[2]

CHR rules the radio today. And radio hasn't been as exciting in years. In New York, Los Angeles, Cincinnati, Houston, Miami, and other major markets, Contemporary Hit Radio (CHR) stations are Number One, generating the massive audience shares and across-the-board demographic profiles that set advertisers' pulses racing. Stations are switching to CHR, big bucks are being attracted (a Houston AM-FM CHR combination sold recently for $36 million), and CHR has become the format other formats watch.

Contemporary Hit Radio, the more practical definition that supplanted the vague if more allusive "Top 40," isn't the most popular format. In sheer number of stations, Country takes the honors. In total listenership, it's Adult Contemporary. But CHR provides the excitement in radio circles.

You might wonder why all that should interest you, the sophisticated frequent record buyer who listens to home-taped cassettes in the car and soured on radio fifteen years ago when the structured Album-Oriented Radio formats began replacing free-form progressive radio. You read music magazines and are sure you have better taste than most of their critics; you're passionate about your music.

CHR isn't even programming at you. The bulk of listeners are not overly concerned with the music and who's perpetrating it; they're casual, occasional tuners-in who like the sound. CHR's rotation structures and relentlessly bright presentation are designed with them in mind, not you the music expert.

[2]Reprint of a magazine article by Ken Barnes, editor of *Radio and Records*. From THE FIRST ROCK AND ROLL CONFIDENTIAL REPORT, by Dave Marsh. Copyright © 1985 by Duke and Duchess Ventures, Inc. Reprinted by permission of Pantheon Books, a Division of Random House, Inc.

Although listening to CHR all day in an office would drive anyone to preprogrammed cassettes or away from music altogether, it is, consumed in proper doses, perhaps the single most satisfying context for hearing music. At the same time, CHR, at its best, mirrors certain key American, democratic attitudes. The basic CHR commandment has always been "Play the hits." The corollary to that proposition is "no matter what they are"—rock, pop, R&B, country, metal, new wave, etc. If a growling prophecy of impending doom, an ode to the joys of masturbation, or a recommendation of hard drugs as an escape from brutal ghetto realities ("Eve of Destruction," "She Bop," and "Cloud Nine," to single out three monster hits) is what people want to hear, then that's what CHR will give them.

CHR is the melting pot format, wherein, theoretically, the cream of other formats form a varied mix of hits. In recent times elements of that mix have been lacking, but nowadays it's reached a more balanced approximation of the ideal.

CHR also reflects the American obsession with what's new. Black radio has always maintained that preoccupation, running records up and down the charts faster than any other format and generally scorning to play oldies. As a result, black music changes constantly, avoiding stagnation and generating a fresh crop of innovations that later become catalysts for pop changes. Lately, CHR has become equally fixated on current records at the expense of oldies, and the longterm effects on music should be far-reaching.

On a CHR station, then, you'll hear a variety of current hits from different genres. There's a democratic process at work in how those songs are chosen, and fuzzy and indirect as it is, it's more reflective of popular taste than the whims of a disc jockey.

New records are added to CHR playlists by program directors (sometimes with input from music directors and consultants, though most of the former are essentially powerless and the latter rarely bother with individual music selections). Factors in the decision include a record's sound (an undemocratic professional opinion) and persuasion by record company and independent promotion people (also undemocratic but inescapable; records have to be sold and radio, far more than any other medium, is how they're sold).

But the most telling evidence for adding a song is track record. That can be, when a record is brand-new, how well the

artist's records have performed previously (has the audience rated them hits?). Once the song's been out a few weeks, its track record switches from past to present—how's it performing at other
stations?—as evaluated primarily from the statistics in trade publications summarizing nationwide radio activity.

There's a herd mentality that frequently comes into play—if
a programmer sees that sixty-eight stations added the new Savage
Cabbage single this week, he may well add it even without evidence that it's ever going anywhere at those sixty-eight stations.
But the consensus syndrome generally works, when combined
with careful follow-up study of readily available data of how a
record performs elsewhere and crucial monitoring of its progress
in the programmer's own market. That process (measured
through phone research; requests; and, once there's stock in the
market, sales) is as close to the will of the people in action as you'll
find in radio or any communications medium.

Local feedback is the main determinant of the song's frequency of airplay, or rotation. Powers (proven hits and massive instant
response records) will come up every two hours or so (the illusion
of hearing the same song four times in fifteen minutes stems from
punching at least four different radio buttons); others are played
less frequently, down to three, four times a day, according to
their response, familiarity, and sound. This last consideration has
been downplayed in present-day CHR, which prides itself on its
eclecticism and seldom worries about playing two females back to
back or two hard rockers in a row or similar seventies solecisms.
But stations do aim for a certain variety and pace, and most do
some day-parting (saving the most raucous rockers for afternoons
and evenings, using the ballads more often in middays, sticking
with the most familiar hits in morning drive).

Rotations are devised with formidable intricacy to meet the
main needs of listeners—that they be pleasantly surprised when
their favorite songs come up and guaranteed of hearing those favorite songs within the short span of a typical tune-in (e.g., driving to or from work). Spontaneity is vital—you never know just
when a song will come up, and the jolt of suddenly punching into
a favorite hit is something a canned tape or record can never
match.

At the same time, rotation establishes the context for hits, the
shared realm of experience that turns music into something more
than a personal fetish. By their omnipresent airplay, radio hits be-

come soundtracks of the times, their plaints and brags and reflections resonating through the national pulse and psyche—"Born in the U.S.A." "When Doves Cry" soared through the summer of '84 the way "A Hard Day's Night" indelibly sealed the summer twenty years before.

CHR's Rocky Road Back

Twenty years ago, Top 40 provided that context for music; now CHR is doing it again. That return to prominence has been a rocky one, plagued with miscalculations and misguided precepts within the format, as well as intensified competition from other formats.

In 1965 Top 40 was about a decade old; the legend is that in the mid-fifties Midwestern radio magnate Tod Storz, upon hearing barroom patrons play the same few songs in succession on a jukebox, decided repeated airings of the most popular songs might be a more productive way to operate a radio station than the prevailing method of random selection from a seemingly infinite record library. By the late fifties, AM giants across the country were pulling down ratings that dwarf any attainable in today's highly competitive markets.

In the mid-sixties, the competition, outside of the monolithic full-service middle-of-the-road institutions like WCCO/Minneapolis, KDKA/Pittsburgh, and KMOX/St. Louis, was still among the Top 40s themselves. KHJ/Los Angeles became the major test market for a format developed at KYNO/Fresno—"Boss Radio," which combined a very tight playlist (thirty numbered songs plus a few extras) with a rigidly executed presentation of jingles, promotions, and condensed DJ patter in carefully plotted sequence. It was enormously successful, blew two traditional Top 40s out of the water, and swept the nation.

But while KHJ and WABC in New York enhanced their slick formats with legendary, gifted air personalities, ensuring an exciting setting for the music, the bandwagon hoppers, as usual in radio, emulated only the superficialities. So by the late sixties there were legions of stations playing thirty records interspersed with rote jingles and DJs dully reading liner cards.

And, while Boss Radio worked fabulously well within Top 40 itself, it helped open the door to some dangerous competition.

The tightened playlist came along just as music exploded in the fertile 1965–68 period marking the ascension of the album-as-art, the era of "Rubber Soul," "Sgt. Pepper," "Are You Experienced?" "Wheels of Fire." Previously all the best rock and many of the R&B songs had been heard on Top 40, but now a sizable portion of the increasingly sophisticated rock audience felt it wasn't being served by the Boss 30.

At the same time, by fortuitous chance, an entire medium lay fallow, open to innovation. Radio companies had been wondering for years just what to do with their FM outlets. The FCC ruled that co-owned FM stations could simulcast no more than 50 percent of their AMs' programming, so owners *had* to come up with new formats. With sophisticated, high-quality stereo receivers coming into play and stereo's overwhelming domination of record sales (by the end of 1967 mono was almost extinct), the solution was at hand. Spurred by pioneers like WOR-FM/New York and KMPX-FM/San Francisco, everything came together as if preordained, and "progressive radio" was born.

At first, it was revelatory to hear album tracks and loads of new artists presented by DJs chatting in groovy hipspeak instead of the Peter Puker phoniness of the Top 40 jocks. As practiced by Top 40 alumni retaining a sense of commercial pacing, like Scott Muni at WOR-FM, progressive radio was a welcome innovation. But the freeform esthetic of DJ's-choice just as often led to sets like the one recalled by author Bruce Pollock: " . . . jugband music, a 16-minute drum solo by Ginger Baker, a two-hour raga by Ravi Shankar, followed by Jimi Hendrix playing 'The Star-Spangled Banner,' Arlo Guthrie's prodigious 'Alice's Restaurant,' . . . Jerry Walker's 'Mr. Bojangles,' *all in succession*" (italics, and an evident though mysterious liking for such indulgences of the airwaves, Pollock's).

But the freeform format, no matter how well it served its hippie audience, was too extreme to attract masses of disenchanted Top 40 fans. After a couple of exposures to the sort of fare depicted by Pollock, they would scurry for the sanctuary of three in a row plus a "More Music" jingle before you could say "In a Gadda Da Vida." Something more commercial was needed, and by the early seventies the format, later to be dubbed AOR (Album-Oriented Radio), was rolling.

AOR was one of the key radio trends that shattered Top 40's dominance in the seventies. It tightened up the music of progressive radio while keeping the hip trappings of presentation (the laid-back, no-hype DJ mode). And it inherited the most valuable legacy of freeform—the idea that FM itself was hip. This conviction was successfully implanted in a generation and will likely never dissipate; it has effectively caused the death of AM as a music medium (although many CHRs managed to migrate to FM early enough to avoid much of the carnage).

Another factor was the rise of Arbitron, which became the leading ratings firm by the turn of the seventies. Radio was growing up—Top 40 and then FM had given new life to a medium written off as moribund when TV came along in the fifties. Now radio's potential was serious business, and as one consequence, the relatively haphazard and generalized ratings services of earlier days (Hooper, Pulse) were supplanted by the detailed diary data of Arbitron, information that was more accurate and more specifically broken out. Demographics became a buzzword— total audience share 12+ was no longer the only consideration that counted. The national ad agencies, whose interest in radio had been reawakened, wanted to know how well stations could deliver 25-34 working females, 18-49 upwardly mobile adults, and so on.

Advertisers' passion for adult demographic cells (25-54 has been their most requested demo for years now), combined with the realization that the country's population bulge was aging and teens were not only less desirable but less numerous, triggered a scramble to raise stations' top-end demos. Many stations moved toward Adult Contemporary (A/C), a modernized easy listening format, believing that listeners who had grown up on rock & roll, were turned off by AOR's hard-rocking ultrahipness, and thought Top 40 was for kids would go for a format that served up the Neil Diamonds and Carole Kings then becoming popular while ditching the Tony Bennetts and Steve and Eydies that the new A/C audience considered square.

So with AOR the new hip format for teens and A/C lopping off the 25-49s, Top 40 was in a bad squeeze. Its reaction, instead of fighting back aggressively, was to roll over and play dead. Research ruled, and the watchword was "what you don't play won't hurt you." It was during the mid-to-late seventies that audiences were defined as "active" (buys records, phones in requests, avid

listener, goes to concerts, knows all the artists' names) vs.
"passive" (casual listener, rarely buys records, doesn't know or
care who's singing what).

This division is not at all inaccurate, but the programming
emphasis was placed almost exclusively on trying to please (or,
more accurately, not to offend) the passives. Playlists tightened
even further, presentations grew blander, music homogenized
and softened and became virtually indistinguishable from A/C.

In 1979 a new mutation complicated matters. The Disco format, riding a trend, exploded in New York with WKTU and
WBLS and in a few other cities. It quickly burned out, thanks to
the radio tradition of quick and shoddy imitations, plus an un-
precedentedly virulent (and, I'm convinced, closet racist) media
assault on the disco phenomenon itself. But Disco pulled Black
Radio out of its low-powered, low-profile ghetto by exposing predominantly black artists to a large (for a while) white audience.
By mixing in compatible white artists, it established a new melting
pot format, this time heavy on the black ingredients.

The successful Disco stations evolved basically by changing
their identities (as soon as "Disco" became poison), first to Dance
Music and then, as a strong funk wave provided some relief from
the metronomic dance beat, to Urban Contemporary. In many
ways, Urban did what Top 40 should have been doing, playing
a wide range of music (rock and pop songs were added, in moder-
ation, into the Urban mix) and drawing top ratings in many markets. Top 40, meanwhile, shrank further, until markets as large
as Houston and St. Louis had no mass appeal hit radio stations at
all.

The CHR Turnaround

But by 1983, the newly rechristened CHR format had re-
versed its decade-long decline and made a dramatic comeback.
The competition helped considerably. AOR fell into a trap of its
own devising, building a core of hard-rocking "earth dogs" (in
AOR's felicitous if unflattering phrase) who resented any attempt
to broaden playlists from a narrow roster of acceptable stadium
rockers. AOR therefore couldn't expand its audience (to more
desirable female and 25+ demographic cells) without blowing off
its 18–24 male core, and its narrow perception of acceptable
AOR music made it, ironically, a highly conservative format.

A/C became even more mossbound, taking the passive-audience "what you don't play won't hurt you" credo to its ultimate extension. Stations increased their oldies quotas, while cutting current playlists to new lows of eight records, only the safest A/C hits, generally added late in their hit lifetimes. While these moves didn't damage A/C stations' ratings or revenues, they did give CHR less direct competition and more room to maneuver.

Urban Contemporary suffered from a variety of problems. Slipshod imitations of successful stations led to quick "abandon format" bailouts. Programmers unfamiliar with the pulses of their markets destroyed the rhythm of some stations, while subpar presentations—often caused by much lower budgets than those enjoyed by white-formatted stations—also hurt. And ad agencies felt that Urban audiences, though often large, were too youthful and economically disadvantaged (a form of racism operated here, too); the resultant sales difficulties convinced some stations to switch to safer, more lucrative formats. Urban also fell prey to cooptation by smart CHR stations, who, once they woke up, found that picking off the cream of the Urban hits could inflict serious ratings damage on their Urban competitors.

MTV has to be given some credit for aiding in CHR's rise, too, although the video channel's reach and influence has been so grossly exaggerated by the TV-oriented and credulous media that I'm reluctant to lavish any more attention on it. For its first year or two (1981–83), MTV was faced with a shortage of programmable videos; it played what it had, which was mostly current material, often by new artists, much of that from England, where videos were already integrated into the pop scene at large. (Now, assured of an ample supply of new videos and possessing a large library of already-played material, it has become more conservative and waits for strong radio airplay before placing any but superstar videos in heavy rotation.) MTV's fostering of new artists did have an effect on CHR, but it dovetailed with the format's own desire to broaden its image and present a livelier, more exciting profile. Another consequence of MTV's advent that's turned out to be beneficial for CHR, one generally overlooked, is the video network's near-complete emphasis on singles. Videos generally aren't even made for album tracks that aren't planned as singles, and MTV, administered by former radio programmers, wants to play the hits. So the interests of MTV and CHR coincide in a way that shuts out, to some degree, AOR (which has become increasingly singles-oriented itself in the past half-decade but is limited by a lack of musical variety even more pronounced than MTV's).

But exterior factors aside, CHR had to wake up to capitalize on the positioning problems of its competition. A lot of credit goes to consultant Mike Joseph, who'd been one of the architects of Top 40 in the sixties with WKNR/Detroit and WABC in New York. Joseph's "new" Hot Hits format, which took off in Philadelphia and St. Louis and Detroit around 1981, was essentially classic Top 40 revisited. The guiding tenet was, once again, "Play the hits," and those hits were selected via traditional methods like tracking sales and requests, not Top 40's random callouts to passives asking them whether they liked songs they'd never heard before on the basis of a muffled fifteen-second excerpt played over the phone. This change of emphasis meant that rockers and black crossovers became acceptable again, since stations weren't so worried about alienating passive listeners, preferring to attract the active "opinion leaders" who tend to spread the word about a hot new station. Hot Hits stations tried to create an atmosphere of excitement; they played a lot of hits, relatively (from forty to fifty-five, counting playlist extras), and insured their frequent rotation by eliminating oldies entirely.

There were also many rigid rules governing jingle placement, DJ presentation, pacing, and the like (shades of Boss Radio), and so many Hot Hits stations and bandwagon jumpers modified the regulations, adding a few oldies (mostly "recurrents," or songs recently departed from the playlist) and tinkering with the mechanics. But playing the hits continued to work, as radio executives realized that the upper end of the 18–34 demographic was not averse to rocking out.

Approaches were refined, as stations like KKBQ-FM/ Houston and WRBQ-FM/Tampa collected monolithic ratings with the innovation of the "Morning Zoo." This wild, almost chaotic morning team concept (featuring a DJ, sports guy, newsperson, character voices, and more) achieved national notoriety when WRBQ-FM PD Scott Shannon imported the concept to his new station, Z-100/New York. It reached the top of the ratings in just two "books" (quarterly ratings periods), breaking a five-year monopoly of Urban Contemporaries at the top of the music station standings. Meanwhile, KIIS/Los Angeles, sparked by morning man Rick Dees, began to pull away from a pack of contemporary competitors (up to nine CHRs plus A/Cs and Oldies stations), gradually building to an unheard-of 10 share (10 percent of the listening audience) by summer 1984, a figure that rivaled, despite having been achieved in a far more competitive era, KHJ's loftiest peaks.

KIIS and Z-100 at the Pinnacle

KIIS and Z-100 are the shining success stories of the CHR format, reigning at Number One in the nation's two top markets. If you had to choose just one leader, both as an achiever and a role model, it would have to be KIIS. Z-100 shot to the top in New York against almost no CHR competition (conservative AM WNBC and FM WPLJ, just switched from almost fifteen years as an AOR), although beating America's three most powerful Urban Contemporaries was no mean feat. But now (as of the fall '84 ratings), WHTZ's grip on the lead is precarious, with WPLJ solid and two more stations, Urban WKTU and AOR WAPP, having switched to CHR for a piece of the action. KIIS, on the other hand, always had competitors galore, and its current 9.1 share doubles that of any other "active music" station (a category excluding news, talk, and easy listening outlets).

Surrounding the Hits

Music is in all likelihood not the most important element of a CHR station's ratings health. In the grand scheme of things, most CHRs play essentially the same music. It's the surroundings, the sizzle, the presentation that makes the difference, that creates an exciting environment in which to hear the hits, that keeps people listening to the radio instead of watching TV or playing tapes and records. The basic ingredients of a successful presentation are on-air energy (jingles, tone of jocks' voices), promotions (flashy contests that hook listeners and smaller-scale recurring on-air bits that relate to listeners—sending logoed coffee mugs to office workers listening to the station on the job, for instance), and personality. The fallout from a generation of liner-card-reading on-air robots has made it difficult for many CHRs (and radio stations in general) to develop a workable personality approach, but almost all agree it's vital to have DJs who generate outrage, sympathy, controversy, laughter, camaraderie, or all those things.

The key to a station's personality image is the morning show, where the heaviest radio listening is focused. Conventional wisdom has it that once listeners are hooked at the start of the day (when they welcome a lighthearted personality approach to ease them into the working grind), they're likely to stay with the same station throughout. Z-100 and KIIS have formidable morning shows for just that purpose.

Z-100's "Morning Zoo" features two longtime prominent DJs, Scott Shannon and Ross Brittain, and a wild, unpredictable, highly topical audio assault of jokes, put-ons, elaborate song parodies, on-air interviews, phony commercials, and other forms of outrageousness. The Zoo also leads the way in sniping at other stations, by name, with an infectious juvenile snideness that keeps listeners wondering just what they'll come up with next. With about four current records an hour played, the emphasis is definitely on the antics of the Zookeepers.

KIIS's Rick Dees combines wit and warmth as well as any air personality in the nation. His staged phone bits can be as crazy (and cruel) as anyone's, and his exchanges with his "agent" are perhaps the wickedest Hollywood satire going. But there's a natural flow (with considerably more music than on Z-100) that prevents the pace from becoming too frantic, and a sense that Dees genuinely likes his job, his on-air cohorts, and his audience—the warmth factor that Z-100 may lack in its frenetic attack on the senses.

But both approaches work superbly in their respective markets (and may reflect the basic personalities of those markets), and provide the foundation for their stations' ratings. Interestingly, neither station displays much personality for the rest of the day, although contests and promotion, request tabulations, and the like keep the stations sounding active.

Will CHR continue to flourish? Radio format successes seem to have a pendulum effect, in part because a format often becomes successful by filling a hole, and once it becomes successful, competitors flock to jump on the bandwagon and the available audience is divided up into smaller slices. So the trend may swing away from CHR, if another format gets its act together sufficiently to wrest the audience away. (Already, with KIIS dropping almost a full point from summer to fall '84—although its margin over the Number 2 station increased by over a point—and Z-100 dropping for two consecutive books, the doomsayers are predicting a CHR nosedive.)

The legion of bandwagon jumpers trying to clone Z-100, KIIS, and the Hot Hits stations could be in for some trouble. It's one thing to tell the morning jock and newsman to work up some goofy banter, call the show "The Zoo," and promo the station as "The Flamethrower" at the top of the hour; it's quite another to put all the elements together as cleverly as Scott Shannon does. KIIS, with the sophisticated demographics-spanning appeal of Rick Dees and its highly responsive music structure, may be even harder to imitate, although probably a superior model for longterm success. Cheap simulations and quickie format-switchers will fall by the wayside in large numbers.

AOR could regain some lost ground by broadening its musical scope and recapturing its former image as the music leader (by playing second and third tracks from albums well in advance of their release as singles, instead of sheepishly waiting as it generally does now). A/C, while not likely to radicalize its approach, could still reap longterm benefits from the aging of the population bulge. And Urban Contemporary, with its energy and exciting blend of music (even more exciting, to my mind, than CHR's usually is), could be CHR's strongest competitor in many markets if it can overcome its economic and image problems.

But CHR's return to the classic tenets of Top 40 has shown that people still want to hear the familiar hits, in a variety of styles, presented attractively. And those rock-bred listeners may be willing to stay with CHR well into their forties.

Assessing CHR's Effects

Meanwhile, the CHR revival is having a healthy and intriguing effect on music. As mentioned earlier, major market CHRs have been quick to coopt big Black/Urban hits (not quick enough, though; many are still paralyzingly slow in adding black records, delaying because of largely unfounded fears of turning off listeners), and that wider exposure can only help black artists. The energetic image sought by CHRs has returned most ballads to the realm of A/C and fostered a livelier brand of CHR hits. CHR has been much more open to new artists than in years past, as playlists have lengthened dramatically (at fifty-two CHRs in the nation's million-plus markets, the average playlist at 1984's end numbered forty-three songs, an increase of about 33 percent in four years).

At the same time it's playing more new artists, CHR is also sticking with its proven artists for a longer time. Nowadays artists like Billy Joel, Lionel Richie, and of course Michael Jackson have been scoring five, six, even seven hits off one album (the almost universal limit used to be three). This development is probably a consequence of CHR's no-oldies stance—top artists generally take two years or more between new albums, and when you don't have the crutch of playing their oldies (except for occasional recurrents), you're tempted to find another track to play from the current album. Record companies and managers then persuade artists to construct albums with up to half a dozen potential singles, which eliminates the two-hits-and-a-lot-of-self-indulgent-filler syndrome and strengthens the overall quality of LPs. CHR's supremacy puts more emphasis on high-quality singles in general, and has thus tightened and brightened up the entire music environment. Most of 1984's best singles—"Jump," "Dancing in the Dark," "Cruel Summer," "Out of Touch," "Time After Time," "Lucky Star," "Boys of Summer," "Run to You," "When Doves Cry"—are tailormade for CHR, and many sound deliberately crafted for the format.

CHR's deemphasis on oldies is an interesting positioning move. It certainly doesn't displease record companies, who are assured of much more airtime for their current releases from new and established artists. The policy also helps isolate CHR from AOR, which finds itself stagnating in catalog material as its receptivity toward new artists narrows and, despite its predominantly singles-oriented present-day approach, is still perhaps overdependent on oldies; and A/C, which has become a 50 percent or more gold format.

CHR is now the place to go for new music, particularly since Urban Contemporary is still limited in number of stations and, to some degree, mass audience appeal. As long as that image remains paramount and a receptive attitude to new music from all genres prevails, CHR should continue to succeed and play a constructive role in promoting a healthy, diverse, dynamic music scene.

AD NAUSEAM: HOW MTV SELLS OUT ROCK & ROLL[3]

Fantasyland

Steve Blacknell is kind of nervous. He runs a hand over his punk-short red hair and jangles his body a bit, loosening up as best he can at the edge of the studio set that is home to video jockeys on the hottest, heaviest network in cable television, MTV. Blacknell's little jangle dance has straightened his striped jacket, and now he fingers the razor-thin leather tie he wears. He has three turquoise earrings. No one seems to be paying much attention to him.

The action on the set is centered on Martha Quinn. Steve has more than a little interest in the proceedings; after Martha finishes her shift, he will audition for the job of the sixth MTV veejay. It's a coveted job, and no one does it with more spunk than Martha, bubbling with enthusiasm today, even after interviewing a soporific Lou Reed. She'd *tried* to pump him up, even attempted to show him how to score points on the Gravitar videogame on the arcade area of the set. But from the moment the cameras rolled and she said, "Watching Gary Numan with me is Lou Reed" (a lie: neither was watching Gary Numan, since MTV videos aren't mixed into the show until it airs seven or so hours later), it was clear that this wouldn't be one of MTV's most dynamic dialogues. A sample:

MARTHA: Did you see the Donald Fagen video?

LOU: Who?

MARTHA: (*unfazed*) Donald Fagen.

LOU: No.

Oh well. Now, as Martha moves around the set, the camera follows her like Robby the Robot in some Fifties movie. Like everything else on MTV, the set is a meticulously designed fantasy. The idea was to create a gestalt of comfy limbo, the basement or rec room of a family that has cared enough to adopt you as one of their own. The furnishings, according to one of the providers, are "the kinds of goodies a fifteen-year-old would want in his

[3]Reprint of a magazine article by contributing editor Steven Levy. From *Rolling Stone.* p30+. D. 8, '83. By Straight Arrow Publishers, Inc. © 1986. All rights reserved. Reprinted by Permission.

bedroom"—stuff like stereo equipment, albums, wooden boxes, videogames and vaguely nifty doodads on the wall, including gold records donated from the likes of Men at Work, Loverboy and Journey. From where Steve sits, near the far wall, it seems there are some books on the shelves, but actually they're cases for videocassette tapes.

Every one of the areas is familiar to the veejays and crew, and has earned its own little nickname. There is a dinerlike counter called "Little Sam's" (named after a nearby coffee shop), "The Jungle" (a few plants), "The Pretzel Chair," "The Kitchenette" (a counter with a little window dropped out), "The Pickle Wall" and "The Barber Chair." Steve Blacknell is hoping that this landscape will be part of his life, too. He's come all the way from England, where he hosts a BBC show, and he can feel in his bones that he's right for this. Blacknell connected with MTV the first time he saw it, in an American hotel room. Those images! And the fact that it goes on and on, twenty-four hours a day! Then Blacknell heard that MTV was still seeking a sixth veejay, even after viewing over a thousand tapes. So here he is.

Martha is bouncing to the music piped in between shots. It's "Billie Jean," by Michael Jackson, a song that had already reached Number One before it was allowed to enter MTV's playlist. "Great tune," she says and does a few voiceovers that wrap up her segment. Now it's Steve's time to audition.

Sitting on a tall stool near the Kitchenette, he runs through some music news, the innocuous tidbits about rock artists that the station provides twice an hour. He's talking too fast, but Julian Goldberg, MTV's executive producer, doesn't seem to mind. "He's got a certain electricity," Goldberg says. This is essential, since the key to MTV is "magic," the ability to overrule logic and get straight to emotion, the better to enhance the commercial environment. The next part of the audition requires Blacknell to elaborate on a few "slugs"—details of a band whose videos have just been shown. Blacknell is able to display considerable musical knowledge here, noting with requisite freshness that a Soft Cell song has remained on the British charts for "an amazing fawty-wun weeks!"

Then he loses it. Stops dead. "My throat's gone," he says. He's given a drink, is asked to try to walk and talk at the same time and is asked to talk about himself for a while. He's thirty years old, a nurse by trade. He's had his successes, but only one thing matters now. The emotion is genuine when he faces that unblinking red light, which has replaced reality with image in the world of rock & roll, and says, "MTV is great. I love it. I want to be a part of it."

Your audition was for naught, Steve—you didn't get the job—but don't despair. You *are* a part of MTV. As is anyone with even the vaguest interest in what rock & roll was, is and will become. Whether they like it or they don't.

MTV is inescapable. Even if you have never watched it, its catalytic effect on the rock industry has probably affected what songs you hear, maybe what records you buy. And its significance goes deeper. MTV is a stunning paradigm for our time and may be a heady portent for our future.

At the very least, MTV is the one network in the cable revolution that has become a phenomenon. Run on the same format and "clock" as a radio station, MTV is always on the air, in stereo for those who pay extra for a hookup to their amplifiers. Like a radio station, it plays a selection of songs and has a small roster of personalities who introduce the songs. Like a radio station, it gets its songs free from record companies, who hope that the exposure will sell records.

But MTV has what radio never had: visions. Some are weird and horrid—bats, banshees, women in bridal dress turning into hideous monsters, glass breaking in slow motion, unruly crowds united in Nazi salute. Others are spacey—airless, impeccably decorated rooms lifted off the pages of *Architectural Digest*, filled with elegant people tearing away at a lush banquet like feral beasts. The visions are driven by rock music—either heavy-metal pounding or synthesizer-driven post–New Wave pop. Together, they create a world of their own, where the shocking image is the norm, where no laws (not even gravity, considering how many people routinely fly up in the air) are enforced, where no taboos remain, where women are young, pouty, gorgeous and slit-skirted and men wear sleeveless T-shirts, pretend to play electronic instruments and are not at all concerned that the instruments are almost never wired or miked.

Powered by these visions, MTV has garnered a loyal audience that supports the songs on MTV by buying records. And although only 16 million homes are connected to cable companies that carry MTV, already the channel has become perhaps the crucial element in the marketing of a rock & roll song. Increasingly, it is becoming a factor in the selection of which rock & roll songs get recorded and which bands get recording contracts at all.

MTV's most stunning achievement has been in domesticating the relatively media-primitive field of rock and in coaxing it into the ultracommercial video arena, where products lose identity as anything but products, where it is impossible to distinguish between entertainment and sales pitch.

MTV has executed its concept brilliantly, taking advantage of the power of video to enhance the scientific, logical, strictly financial aspect of the music business. This has been accomplished by MTV's construction of an atmosphere that creates an artificial sense of community, jars the senses and appeals to the subconscious of well-to-do rock fans.

MTV is perfect for a generation never weaned from television, because its videos contain few lines between fantasy and reality. Sexual fantasies blend with toothless gossip about a rock community that really does not exist, having dissipated maybe a decade ago. It doesn't matter. There are no dissenting opinions or alternative views telecast on MTV. Profit-making television creates an unreal environment to get people into what is called a "consumer mode"; MTV, as its executives boast, is pure environment. It is a way of thought, a way of life. It is the ultimate junk-culture triumph. It is a sophisticated attempt to touch the post-Woodstock population's lurking G spot, which is unattainable to those advertisers sponsoring *We Got It Made*.

It is easy to get lost in the fun-house environment of MTV, to spend idle hours in a dull stereo stupor, watching video clips and Martha Quinn, without glimpsing what is behind the visions with which MTV so relentlessly provides us. Behind the funhouse mirror is another story, one that makes the musical energy and optimism of the Sixties seem a thousand light-years ago. After watching hours and days of MTV, it's tough to avoid the conclusion that rock & roll has been replaced by commercials.

Whose MTV Is It, Anyway?

Pete Townshend strides toward the camera with the confidence of a practiced stage performer. He looks ticked off. There is righteous anger in his voice. "Call your cable operator now," Townshend implores. "Call him and say, 'I want my Em Tee

Vee!'" It's a convincing message: after commercials like this (also featuring such noted pitchmen as Stevie Nicks, Mick Jagger, Pat Benatar and Adam Ant) were shown on noncable stations in markets like Los Angeles, cable operators were bombarded with letters and calls from rock fans demanding "their" MTV.

Indeed, America's youth are possessive about MTV. Research in Middle American outposts like Tulsa, Wichita, Peoria, Grand Rapids, Syracuse and Houston shows that once people in that exalted target demographic of fourteen to thirty-four tune in to MTV (median age: twenty-four), they watch it fanatically, almost five days a week, averaging well over an hour a day. The veejays on MTV are always impressed when, on promotional forays into the hinterland, they are swamped by hundreds of well-wishing fans who, says one veejay, would probably turn out if they heard "that the mail-room guy of MTV was showing up—they just want to be a part of it."

All of this pleases . . . Bob Pittman, executive vice-president and chief operating officer of Warner Amex Satellite Entertainment Company (WASEC), who was the driving force behind MTV. "People in Podunk, Iowa, think it's more theirs than it is mine. It's a cult."

Just the way Bob Pittman planned it. Pittman, whose name is most often amended with the epithet *Wunderkind*, is an extremely articulate, conservatively dressed twenty-nine-year-old who has been in the radio and television end of the music business since he was fifteen. His style is informal, within the bounds of corporate decorum. His meteoric career has been characterized by a penchant for market research and a willingness to discard traditional "wisdom" in favor of pursuing the "real meaning" of the data compiled by phone calls, sales-trend analyses and surveys of the Mood of the Nation: "What's going on in people's lives, and how can we fit into it?"

"Our core audience is the television babies who grew up on TV and rock & roll," Pittman says. "The strongest appeal you can make [to these TV and rock babies] is emotionally. If you can get their emotions going, [make them] forget their logic, you've got'em."

This goes hand in hand with Pittman's contention that music is "100 percent mood and emotion." With MTV, he set out to "amplify the mood and include MTV in the mood." Every component of MTV, from the clever promotional animations to the personalities of the veejays, is designed to "create more of the mood that's appealing," so that "the appeal of MTV is greater than the sum of its parts."

But before any of this was put into effect, WASEC did extensive market research, first on the feasibility of the channel and then on the kinds of appealing moods that rock fans wanted amplified.

"We believe [MTV] was the most researched channel in history," boasts Marshall Cohen, who was formerly in charge of WASEC research and is now vice-president of programming and marketing services. First, 600 fourteen- to thirty-four-year-olds were interviewed to determine if there was interest in such a channel. An astounding eighty-five percent responded positively. Cohen then embarked on a "market-segmentation study": the names of over 150 musical artists were floated to see who would be the superstars and pariahs of MTV. This study also probed the lifestyle of potential rock-video consumers to find out, says Cohen, "the way the channel should feel, the image, the style, what the veejays should wear—should they wear suits or punk clothes?"

WASEC also did surveys of cable operators and, more informally, advertising agencies and record companies, which would be the "clients" and "suppliers" of this new service. Response was generally favorable, but some record companies wanted payment in return for lending their video clips to MTV. Bob Pittman and Carolyn Baker (who, at the time, was MTV's director of talent and acquisitions) set about doing a sales job on these holdouts to convince them that, in essence, MTV was telecasting free commercials for record albums. "If you look at our [advertising] rate card," says Pittman, "we're giving them a million dollars' worth of exposure for a hit song." This argument convinced all but a few of the record companies (notably MCA and Polygram), and the holdouts came in from the cold when they realized that the clips did indeed work like commercials when it came to selling records.

Armed with this research data and his original concepts (which were worked out with then executive vice-president of WASEC, John Lack), Pittman and a small crew of executives set out to create the mood and emotion that would be MTV. Although the features of MTV *seemed* like direct cops from radio's format, there were careful adjustments for maximum visual effect and psychological impact. Whereas most radio stations report the news for public-service reasons, MTV decided to do only music news because, says Pittman, in the fourteen- to thirty-four-year-old music culture, "knowledge is status." Whereas radio stations hold contests to get more listeners, MTV holds its contests "to help build an emotional bond through the fantasies they develop," says Pittman.

John Sykes, MTV's programming head, elaborates: "Promotion is key," he says. "[We wanted] MTV almost larger than life when we started, so we had to have grand fantasy promotions. Everything had to have a weird edge to it. *Any* station can give a trip to Hawaii, but we offered a luau with Pat Benatar. Zany ideas, but there's a method to the madness: good marketing plan, strong rotation for announcements, entries in record stores . . . it means our viewers are involved in MTV."

The look of the studio "wraparound" segments was painstakingly crafted by Pittman's executive producer, Sue Steinberg, and creative director, Bob Morton (both of whom left MTV on amicable terms after the channel went on the air). The set had to be an "anything could happen here" kind of place, says Steinberg. After rejecting "everything from flashy space-age to modular high-tech," they finally settled on the now classic loftlike backdrop.

Hiring veejays was not so easy. Pittman wanted MTV to have "good guides who could sublimate their egos, be human faces you could relate to." After thousands of candidates—everyone from street people to soap-opera stars—provided tapes, were interviewed and/or went through auditions, five veejays were selected: Nina Blackwood, a punkish blond actress from L.A. ("young-looking, sexy, hip . . . the young boys will go nuts," Steinberg predicted); J. J. Jackson, a black deejay who'd once held court in Boston's top "underground" FM station, WBCN; Mark Goodman, a jock from WMMR in Philadelphia (Steinberg: "a teen-idol-type—we hoped young girls would write letters, start fan clubs . . ."); Alan Hunter, a struggling actor from Mississippi; and Martha Quinn, the stepdaughter of pop economist Jane Bryant Quinn.

Though Martha's on-camera experience had been limited to commercials for the likes of McDonald's and Kellogg's, her energy translated instantly to the MTV format, where one ideally delivers a brief item about somebody's nose job as if it's fun and earth-shattering at the same time.

Martha was just out of college and had little music-business experience beyond liking rock. But that didn't matter; she had "magic." The veejays' connection to the music was to be symbolic; they would have no say at all in what videos were chosen or the order in which they were shown. During off-hours, they would have to study clips in an office called the "VJ Lounge" so that they could comment on them during studio stints, perpetuating the myth that the show was live. (In fact, the only live presence as the videos are being aired is the technical director at the "uplink facility" in Smithtown, Long Island, who sits at a console beside a Rolodex that lists the opening and closing shots of every video clip and promo in the MTV library. The technical director consults a playlist and provides a proper visual segue from clip to clip, sometimes splitting the screen and bleeding one clip into the next, other times spinning the screen à la *Star Wars*.)

While the wraparound plans were under way, Bob Pittman was narrowing down the musical limits of MTV. He has never been one to believe in the "golden gut" theory of programming, in which some exalted self-proclaimed genius feels a hit deep in his belly and inks it on top of the playlist. He believes in input from the people. Let MTV be a democracy like all of America! Freedom of choice!

So MTV would begin its equivalent of the Nielsen ratings, which have done so much to elevate the quality of broadcast television. Each night, at least five full-time telephone surveyors would make phone calls to residents of areas that received MTV—as many as 5000 calls a week. After ascertaining that someone was between fourteen and thirty-four and watched MTV, they would pound the poor viewer with questions: "Are you familiar with the clip by Styx called 'Mr. Roboto'? Let me play it for you." Then the song would be played over the phone and the viewer probed until somehow, a rating would be awarded from one to ten, each number representing something on the scale from "Can't stand it" to "I like it, but I'm seeing a bit too much of it" (Burnout! Burnout! Bane of the programmer!) to "Can't get enough of it." These results are considered—along with a record's sales performance and the response to a song in rock clubs—to determine where a given clip fits in the format: whether the song will be played in "heavy rotation" (an average of four times a day), "medium rotation" (two to three times a day), "light rotation" (around once a day), in any of various other formats or dropped entirely.

Of course, not *any* old video clip gets on MTV. The MTV format is strictly limited to Bob Pittman's definition of "rock & roll," as revealed by his advance work. His research showed that mixing in country music, R&B or wimpy Top Forty hits like Barry Manilow would turn off his main target audience. But he vowed to give a chance to any rock video that met MTV's technical standards and didn't "show naked women running around or throwing babies out of trucks." MTV isn't in the job of making value judgments on its video clips.

But when MTV went on the air on August 1st, 1981, it still didn't look right to Pittman. After all the work to make it look like it was as natural and informal as the rock culture itself, MTV still seemed like *television*. Veejays would read their scripts off teleprompters, then stare at the camera like deer transfixed by headlights.

Drastic steps were taken. "Get rid of these bright, phony lights!" the MTV people said, ordering [inferior] lighting instead. The teleprompters went as well. Veejays were instructed to ad-lib from basic scripts, to relax more and to stop worrying about making mistakes. Mistakes would look *real*. It took a little while, but MTV finally got what it wanted—a well-designed studio that looked like something casually thrown together, scripted patter that sounded like it was made up on the spot, an ironclad format that proceeded like a random chain of events, well-trained actors who came on like folks you'd meet at a campus mixer, and a generally perfectionist attitude in bringing about a what-the-hell-let's-boogie mood.

It worked.

Marshall Cohen did a quick research study and found that the people watching MTV were precisely the fourteen- to thirty-four's that had been targeted—the initial studies had been "right on the money." Even better was the *way* in which these viewers were watching. Instead of catching a random clip here and there, viewers were tuning in specifically to watch MTV, and once they tuned in, they would watch it for a while. "We thought MTV would be secondary to television," says Pittman, "but our research showed that people watched it seventy percent more intently. MTV turned out to be even more hypnotic."

The spell was binding: MTV viewers flooded the station with mail, some letters directed at the veejays (Nina got soulful poetry, Mark got mash notes from young girls), others asking for more

Journey or April Wine. Within a year, the volume of viewer mail approached 100,000 pieces a month.

Of course, by that time, MTV's audience had grown. Cable operators saw the wisdom in including a well-targeted youth service among their offerings, especially since MTV gave operators two minutes of free ad time each hour (which they could resell) and a potential gold mine in the stereo hookup (which costs subscribers about two dollars a month). Carried by about 1775 cable operators two years after its launch, MTV is the fastest-growing cable network in history.

Even more amazing was the effect MTV was having on record sales. From the start, MTV had promised the record companies they would see benefits from airing their promo clips on the channel; when Pittman was cornered into predicting when these benefits would accrue, he promised that results would be clear within a couple of years. As it turned out, *six weeks* after MTV went on the air, record sales of certain artists in heavy rotation started to rise in places saturated by MTV, like Tulsa, Oklahoma.

Especially remarkable was the kind of artist who experienced these sales boosts. Since MTV played more new music than many AOR radio stations and was particularly willing to give a shot to new English artists armed with striking videos, acts like Adam Ant, Human League and Duran Duran got much of their initial national exposure through MTV airplay.

And like any good television commercial, the videos had their effect—MTV viewers went out and bought the records. You could almost make a tactical map of the country, darken the MTV areas and see the sales of certain records increasing in those areas. Kids in Middle American cities like Des Moines asking for records that had never been played on the local radio. Oingo Boingo selling in Newport News, Virginia. A Flock of Seagulls selling in Lawton, Oklahoma. The Clash being requested in Boise, Idaho. A Nielsen survey commissioned by MTV early this year quantified this effect—sixty-three percent of MTV viewers said that MTV influenced their record-buying decisions. MTV viewers averaged nine album buys a year, and four of those purchases were influenced by what they had seen on the channel.

MTV was justifiably proud of its successful promotion of a new subgenre of music it calls "modern pop"—the fresh, visually oriented and culturally harmless groups like the Stray Cats and Men at Work, whose emergence as "megastars" (Pittman's term) was primarily due to MTV exposure. But even though MTV's format was freer than that of AOR, they shared the same flaw: their purpose was not to provide the best, most challenging music possible, but to ensnare the passions of Americans who fit certain demographic or, as Pittman puts it, "psychographic" requirements—young people who had money and the inclination to buy things like records, candy bars, videogames, beer and pimple cream.

This was the essence of the "narrowcasting" principle (designing programming with a select audience in mind). It was good business but bad politics, especially since, in practice, it just about eliminated the chances of certain artists' appearing on MTV. Particularly black artists. While MTV vowed to play anything that was rock & roll, its definition of the genre seemed to include very few black artists: of the over 750 videos shown on MTV during the channel's first eighteen months, fewer than two dozen featured black artists, even including such racially mixed bands as the English Beat. When videos by black artists were submitted, MTV would reject them, claiming they were not "rock & roll" songs.

There were repercussions. Rick James, whose popular, rock-styled "Super Freak" was rejected by MTV, called the channel racist and charged that MTV set black people back 400 years. Equally firm criticism came from others in the music industry. Journalists and critics quickly identified racism as *the* MTV "issue"; the *San Francisco Examiner* led off its feature section one day with a long piece entitled, "Where Are the Blacks on MTV?"

MTV's response? It's the format! Programming vice-president Les Garland, yet another young, gregarious white executive who wears the jacket and tie required by WASEC informal corporate policy, has a little presentation he gives journalists to explain MTV's format. On a sheet of yellow legal paper, he draws a horizontal line representing the spectrum of popular music. He identifies MTV's format as falling slightly left of center, between AOR (Def Leppard) and modern pop (Men at Work, Talking Heads). On the right are the verboten R&B and country music. Apparently research shows that a soulful excursion with Marvin Gaye or a country fling with Waylon Jennings evokes "strong negatives" in MTV folk: *What's that stuff doing on my MTV?*

This type of explanation sounded rational, but it fell apart simply by evidence of MTV's playlist. Why can Phil Collins sing the Supremes' "You Can't Hurry Love" on MTV while Motown acts get no exposure? Why are Hall and Oates singing black-flavored music on such heavy MTV rotation? Even the powerless veejays seemed embarrassed by the contradictions in the format. A striking example of this occurred early this year, when veejay Mark Goodman was interviewing David Bowie in the superstar's New York hotel room. Bowie asked Goodman if, after the interview, he might turn the tables: he had some "punishing" questions to ask him about MTV. A partial transcript of that conversation shows that Bowie had clearly identified the key issues.

BOWIE: I'm distraught by the fact that there are so few black artists featured [on MTV]. Why is that?

GOODMAN: I think we're trying to move in that direction. We seem to be doing music that fits into what we want to play on MTV. The company is thinking in terms of narrowcasting. . . .

BOWIE: There seem to be a lot of black artists making very good videos that I'm surprised aren't used on MTV.

GOODMAN: Of course, also we have to try and do what we think not only New York and Los Angeles will appreciate, but also Poughkeepsie or the Midwest. Pick some town in the Midwest which would be scared to death by Prince, which we're playing, or a string of other black faces, or black music. . . .

BOWIE: Isn't that interesting.

GOODMAN: We have to play music we think an entire country is going to like, and certainly we're a rock & roll station. . . . We grew up in an era where the Isley Brothers meant something to me. But what does it mean to a seventeen-year-old?

BOWIE: . . . I'll tell you what the Isley Brothers or Marvin Gaye means to a *black* seventeen-year-old, and surely he's part of America.

GOODMAN: No question, no question. That's why we're seeing those things.

BOWIE: Don't you think it's a frightening predicament [for MTV] to be in?

GOODMAN: Yeah. But less so here than in radio.

BOWIE: Don't say, "Well, it's not me, it's them." Is it not possible it should be a conviction of the station and of the radio stations to be fair? . . . Should it not be a challenge to make the media more integrated?

The fact is, MTV had a chance early on to meet that challenge. Before MTV's 1981 launch date, there was considerable in-house argument about what constituted a fair definition of rock & roll. Some employees were convinced, as Goodman admitted to David Bowie, that it was not musical considerations that led Bob Pittman to place songs in the forbidden R&B category, but a fear of alienating the white kids in the suburbs, who, according to research, didn't like black people or their music. "In creating a broad, new area of communication, you shouldn't perpetuate what was wrong in the past," says Carolyn Baker. "I voiced my opinion to Bob—we all talked about it. Bob comes from radio, and I think he wanted the channel to work. . . . He knew what they wanted was an AOR channel.

'The AOR audience is not conducive to black music. Cable's in the suburbs.' Yadda yadda yadda."

While Pittman received these objections cordially, he dismissed them as "ignorant." He feels the criticism the channel has received is at best a misunderstanding of how MTV operates. What he does not realize is that the misunderstanding is only natural, since he has crafted MTV to look like an irreverent, warm kind of place where the musical redlining of black people would not be tolerated. Not like a place where Ronald Reagan's values are more honored than John Lennon's.

When Pittman gets going on the black issue, his speech is peppered with profanities. How can MTV be called racist? It's the format, that's all!

Some people might argue with your definition of rock & roll, Bob.

"Our definition is not speculation. There's a million dollars' worth of research there."

But the power of MTV has made this a bread-and-butter issue for black artists.

"It's *our* bread and butter. If anyone says we should change, I'd like them to take our losses. I'd change our losses with theirs right now. They don't recognize that this is a business. Bloomingdale's wouldn't work if it carried every kind of clothing ever made. MTV is a phenomenon of the youth culture. Our point of view must be hitting home."

Some say that's because, while you may not be racist, you're catering to white suburban racism. And that you're in a position to change that, to expose people to great black artists as well as white ones.

"I don't know who . . . these people are to tell people what they *should* like," Pittman fumes. "They sound like little Hitlers or people from Eastern-bloc communist countries. The good thing about America is that people rule. That's the essence of America!"

But it was not "the people" who designed the format of MTV. It was Pittman and his assistants. Bob Pittman's neck was already out on a $30-million-a-year limb, and he was not about to argue with the executives of Warner Communications, American Express and Warner Amex that maybe profit could wait an extra year until MTV could educate the public about what black artists had to offer.

But MTV did change. Significantly, it was a threat to that eventual profit margin that broke the color line. While black artists like the Bus Boys and Prince had their videos shown, true crossover giants—blacks who fit solidly into a rock context as well as into R&B—had never gotten substantial play on MTV. Pittman insists this was because those artists had always made videos of the "wrong" songs on their albums—cuts that were more R&B than MTV. Then came Michael Jackson.

Jackson's *Thriller* was the best-selling album in the country. MTV was getting nailed coast to coast for ignoring black artists. Black organizations were making noises that they might strike where MTV was vulnerable—the cable operators. Some big urban cable operations were going to open up in the next few years, and the city councils that oversee these operations might not look kindly on those operators who carried a music-video channel with a racist reputation. Arcane arguments about format might not wash in a heated political atmosphere. How could any "format" justify excluding the hottest rock record in the country?

Limelight Productions, which had produced dozens of MTV's most popular videos, had one "Billie Jean" for Jackson's *Thriller* LP. It was a fantastic video, sparked by Jackson's electrifying dance movements. Epic-CBS Records submitted the clip to MTV. The widespread rumor has it that CBS Records threatened to pull all its clips from MTV unless it aired "Billie Jean." MTV and CBS have denied this officially, but it was clear that this was the showdown. Inside MTV, employees urgently prodded their bosses to go with it. "I think we all wanted to see 'Billie Jean' on the channel," says veejay J. J. Jackson.

And it happened. In early March, "Billie Jean" went into heavy rotation, followed by "Beat It," another of the singles off Jackson's record. And suddenly, MTV's playlist seemed a bit more reflective of the fact that blacks make music, too. Of course, MTV claims that by this time, more blacks were making videos slanted toward their requirements. Back in early February, the only blacks on the sixty videos listed on the MTV playlist were Tina Turner (in light rotation) and the English Beat (in medium). But after Michael Jackson's videos were telecast, this changed: by the end of April, the list had eleven black acts, three of which (the two Jackson clips and one by Prince) were in heavy rotation.

Very few of MTV's viewers probably noticed anything different. But then, discerning the machinations of the puppet masters in the elaborate MTV marionette show is a difficult task. Much easier to slip into the netherworld of the video clips—the visions that give MTV its substance. As in the formation of the wraparound segments, there is a story behind the clips, too.

The World according to MTV

A short, blond singer in a leather jacket sits by the edge of a spacious indoor pool. He holds a large knife. We see lots of closeups of the knife. Intercut with this are views of a supple young woman disrobing in a changing stall. Meanwhile, the singer's band plays away at the bottom of the empty pool. The song they mime to is compact and tough. The quick cuts from the knife to the woman (here's a patch of flesh, then another) create a sense of menace. Will the singer slash her? We get our best view yet of the woman as she slips into a tiny black bathing suit. As the instrumentalists pound at their guitars, keyboard, drums, we see the spacious reaches of this deco gymnasium. Now, the woman is at the end of a diving board. Is she going to jump into the empty pool and splatter that rich womanflesh in a gross puddle? There's a painstaking closeup as her feet leave the board. Finally, we see her emerge from the empty pool, soaking wet. The music is ending. The singer with the knife is meeting her by the changing stall. Superimposed on the MTV screen is the data about the video: Bryan Adams, *Cuts like a Knife, A&M Records.*

The world of rock video is in stark contrast to the bland studio where the MTV veejays form emotional bonds with their viewers. The bizarre is the norm here: a world that makes Oz look like Scarsdale. Though MTV does not, of course, make or even pay for the videos, these promotional clips provide the meat of the channel's programming. MTV executives emphasize that "the music is the star."

Two years ago, most of the clips were "performance"-based, with the artist lip-syncing his or her way through a song. Only about thirty percent were "concept" videos, which told a little story along with the music. That ratio has nearly switched, and most of the videos are now better- and bigger-budgeted than they were two years ago. And with good reason.

A successful video, especially when shown in heavy rotation on MTV, can sell a lot of records and easily make back the average production cost of $30,000 to $40,000. (Some videos are made for as little as $15,000; others, like Billy Joel's "Allentown," are in the six-figure range. Michael Jackson's new "Thriller" video, directed by Jon Landis, reportedly cost $500,000.) In some cases, like that of the Stray Cats, Duran Duran and Greg Kihn, videos have boosted careers. Kihn had been suffering mediocre album sales for years, until he made a video of his song "Jeopardy," which portrayed holy matrimony as akin to being body-snatched by some horrid beast. Within three weeks, MTV stuck it in heavy rotation. Sales of the album and the twelve-inch single, both released with the words AS SEEN ON MTV printed directly on the jacket, have "tripled anything Greg's netted so far," says Randy Edwards, a vice-president at Elektra-Asylum. He attributes that to MTV: "Greg's a good-looking guy. It was a good video, and it helped us quite a bit."

The story gets repetitive. "I'd say MTV was a major part of the success of the Stray Cats and directly responsible for the sale of close to half a million albums before the band had any real radio exposure," says Clay Baxter of EMI America Records.

"Adam Ant owes a major part of his success to MTV," says International Creative Management senior vice-president Tom Ross.

That sentiment is echoed by Epic's Glen Brunman. "When you hear that AOR stations are being swamped with calls for Adam Ant's 'Goody Two Shoes' and the only place kids could be hearing it is on MTV, you know there's an impact," says Brunman.

Norman Hunter, a buyer for the 145-store Record Bar chain, says, "I credit MTV totally for the success of Men at Work." He also believes that MTV is the main reason for Duran Duran's success—an observation confirmed by IRS Records' Michael Plen, who thinks that MTV's continued exposure of Duran Duran's "Girls on Film" video made the band into "MTV's biggest success story this year."

On the other hand, a bad video can hurt a band. One record-company executive glumly tells of the performance video made by a heavy-metal band on that company's label. The video showed, all too clearly, that while this contingent sounded like Young Turks, they were, in fact, pot-bellied, balding and getting up in years. "MTV played the hell out of it and sales went *down*," he says. "I wanted to call up and tell them to stop playing the thing."

While rock-video producers see the process as a creative one, they harbor no illusions about what they're doing: making a sort of commercial. (In the case of video clips like "WarGames" or "Maniac," which are literally movie trailers set to music, it's difficult to see the difference between the clip and a commercial.) And although many fans assume that the rock bands are the creative forces behind the videos, that situation is rare. Most often it is the producer, director or record-company exec who works up the concept. These producers readily admit, as does Simon Fields, producer of over 200 clips, that "the purpose of the video clip is to sell the soundtrack."

"I don't think you can be a real artist while dealing in video clips," says producer Paul Justman, who's worked with the J. Geils Band, the Cars and Diana Ross. "Your limitation is the audience, the song and the money. If you try 'serious' work, it won't sell."

The first rule is to grab attention and sustain it. "*Keep the interest*—that's an obsession with us," says John Weaver, whose KEEFCO production company has done over 500 clips, from Paul McCartney to Blondie. "We know why people are turned on or turned off. You've got to keep their attention—create movement where there isn't any. Keep the rhythm. Eliminate any visual slack. We measure in IPMs—ideas per minute. If you keep up your IPM, you'll do all right."

This mania for attention leads producers into an endless search for offbeat themes and startling images. Since most clips are done in a hurry, producers usually rely on familiar concepts. Often, a promo *auteur* will cleverly ape the look of a certain movie, photo or painting. Or, as MTV's John Sykes notes, a particularly disconcerting or spectacular shot might work as a "visual hook" that makes you watch a clip repeatedly, anxious to see that shot again.

Despite the brief history of video clips, many shots have managed to become miserably tired clichés. "Fancy editing, cutaway, flash dissolves, slow motion, double-trick fadeaways going into solarization . . . , man, give me some slack," says Van Halen's lead singer and video star David Lee Roth. "It's still some jerk dancing, lip-syncing the words to a song about 'baby, baby, baby.' This thing of standing next to the Venetian blinds with the light coming through, making bars on your face . . . how many times have you seen that in the last two hours on MTV?"

A new visual hook is a real blessing for directors, and they are quick to complain when the same thing then appears in ten other videos. "I did Rainbow's 'Stone Cold' video with mirrors around the lead singer, and then six months later, I saw the exact technique in the Flock of Seagulls thing," says Ken Walz, who's done videos for Novo Combo, Jon Butcher Axis and others.

The surest shortcut to memorable videos seems to be a liberal dose of sex, violence or both. Outright gore, straight nudity and overtly gruesome situations will lead MTV to ban certain videos (the Rolling Stones' "Neighbors," with body parts stuffed into trunks, for instance), or send them back to the record companies for reediting (Golden Earring's "Twilight Zone" needed a few splices to get rid of bare breasts and a hypodermic needle penetrating skin). But the standards on violence and suggestive sex are fairly loose. Dr. Thomas Radecki, chairman of the National Coalition on TV Violence, says, "It troubles me seriously. Obviously it's similar to regular-programming violence—it sanctions real violence."

Sue Steinberg, former executive producer of MTV, has more specific objections: "The violence to women. Women being pushed away. Spike heels and dark stockings. The emphasis on certain images contributes to the illusion of violence and sexism. They seem to see how far they can go. And it's getting worse."

There is an official MTV line about the violence and sexism: it's only rock & roll. "It's not the Barry Manilow channel," says Bob Pittman. "Some songs are unhappy. Some have a dark message. It's the essence of rock. It mirrors the issues of people moving from adolescence to adulthood."

The clips aren't sexist?

"I think video clips *spoof* sexism. There're a lot of women walking down the street with garter belts—that's absurd. I think people are playing with the theme and making fun of it. We accept total responsibility for what we play. We wouldn't show a sexist clip."

Some producers blame it on the song. Says Ken Walz, "I did a clip for Dr. Hook for a song called 'Baby Makes Her Blue Jeans Talk.' What can you do with a song like that? We had to have a great-looking girl . . . walking down the street."

Others use Pittman's "tongue in cheek" defense. "When we did the Geils Band's 'Centerfold,' the obvious thing was go for the fantasy you had in school—you always wanted to see the girls in slips and bras," says Paul Justman. "So I put a lot of girls in slips and bras." While the "Centerfold" promo does make its point about fantasies, it still has titillating shots of half-naked women—isn't that having your cake and eating it, too? "Yeah," admits Justman. "But no sense in getting too serious about it. It was meant to be humorous."

The same kind of after-the-fact rationale applies to rock-video violence. Take that Bryan Adams clip with the swimming pool, the knife and the girl taking off her clothes. Bob Pittman considers it a Hitchcockian tour de farce. "The artist is trying to create suspense," he says. "I don't think it's antisocial or negative."

Steve Barron of Limelight Productions wrote and directed that video. His assessment of it is not as high as Pittman's. "It's not going on my show reel," he sheepishly admits. Barron's instructions prior to making the video were to establish Bryan Adams as a tough guitar rocker. The single from the album was another song, a relatively mellow ballad, and A&M wanted a video of "Cuts like a Knife" to dispel any notion that Adams was a wimp. "The record company told me it wanted to see the band playing and wanted Adams to have a certain image—not puny. So we needed an earthy, gritty story line. The girl changing made it sexy. The knife was the twist to build tension."

This does not sound like a highroad approach, Steve.

"These things are for promotion. We're not dealing with art students—we're dealing with an average audience in the Midwest."

"Cuts like a Knife" was a wildly successful clip. Bryan Adams called MTV a "godsend" for helping "make my record happen" but recognized that "the most important thing [it did] for me was establish my look." It's becoming commonplace; much as a politician hires a media consultant to give him a certain image, record companies are taking advantage of the videomakers' expertise to develop images for their artists.

The "marketing plan" mentality, in terms of album covers, choice of singles and other considerations, has been in the music industry for a while. But the power of video—"the most powerful selling tool we've ever had," croons Polygram vice-president Len Epand—gives this approach even more potency.

"A video has an effect on a viewer's perception of the artist," says Buzz Brindle, MTV's director of music programming. "If you have an expectation in terms of the artist, this can be changed if the video gives you something different." Brindle cites a recent Journey clip. Though always a popular MTV band, Journey had done mostly macho, performance-style clips. But, perhaps sensing danger in sticking to the group's image as tough-guy purveyors of "dinsoaur" rock, the band sought new audiences. Their recent video has a classier feel. The band members wear tuxedos.

In 1968, we had the "new" Nixon. In 1983, the "new" Journey. Which is the "real" Journey? Does it matter? In the pre-MTV world, we used to construct our own fantasies to music, provide our own images rich in personal meaning. Now, mass images are provided for us. And the primary criterion for choosing these images is not artistic validity or even what the songwriter had in mind, but what might sell the song. MTV and the advertisers who fund the service hope that the effect of these rock images will be to put us into the mood to buy anything that comes to our attention, from chewing gum to MTV satin jackets, yours for only a modest $49.95. MTV has turned rock & roll songs into advertising jingles.

The MTV Coalition

J. J. Jackson is the dean of the veejays. He has a pedigree: during the Sixties, when he spun discs for Boston's pioneering underground FM station WBCN, he was one of the first American deejays to play Led Zeppelin. Those were freewheeling times, where the assumption was that rock music was a catalyst for an artistic ethic that rejected commercialism. If it felt good, say it or play it.

When asked to cite something—anything—of substance that he's said on MTV, J.J. thinks for a while. Finally, he recalls a thought he had about concert audiences—that if you really get into the concert, not just sit back and let others do the clapping, the concert can be a great experience all around. But before J.J. felt free to share this epiphany with MTV's target audience, he felt compelled to "clear it" with his bosses. Wasn't that embarrassing for a mature veteran of free-form Sixties underground radio?

"I try not to look back," says Jackson. "When the Sixties went, I left the Sixties, too."

MTV is an excellent place to study how far we've gone since the Sixties. Listen to Bob Pittman on the rock & roll audience: "In the Sixties, politics and music fused. But there are no more political statements. The only thing rock fans have in common is the music—that's the coalition [that MTV has gathered]."

This is astute social commentary. In the last ten years, there has been no unifying force in rock music. Certainly no common ground where fans of the Clash, Loverboy and Rickie Lee Jones can meet. Yet by utilizing something that almost all young rock fans have in common—television—MTV has gathered the remnants of the rock culture. Unlike the activist Sixties rock coalition, the MTV coalition is essentially passive. Their function is to sit still, watch the commercials and buy the products, not change the world. MTV has gained its power by the ability to befriend this new coalition and exploit it.

MTV will perform studies on this upscale youth audience to prove its willingness to spend money on records and other products. The record companies will keep producing videos for MTV, and the videos will get better and better as the competition for spots in MTV's rotation increases; as the videos get better, the audiences will likely pick up. As the audience picks up, the advertising community—which is only slowly awakening to the sales potential of MTV's well-defined demographics—will probably buy in more heavily: MTV has six minutes of national advertising available each hour and hopes that eventually this time will be solidly booked.

Even more cable operators, enticed by the two free minutes of local advertising available each hour, will begin to carry MTV. Each cable operator brings thousands of potential viewers who want their MTV. The audiences will grow even more, and the process will snowball. "It's going to feed on itself," says Jay James, a senior vice-president at Doyle Dane Bernbach and one of MTV's earliest supporters in the advertising community. "I don't think we've seen the beginning of how successful it's going to be."

MTV people share James' optimism, of course. But even though it has won the music industry's heart, MTV's success is not guaranteed. MTV's raison d'être—profit—is years away, though the head of Warner Amex, former Reagan cabinet member Drew Lewis, hopes it to go in the black in a year. With its relatively small audience, MTV can now charge no more than $1000 to $1500 per minute for most of its commercials; even so, Madison Avenue, as MTV had expected, has been slow to accept the new medium. According to one executive, MTV costs Warner Amex around $30 million a year; revenues covered only half of that last year. No one expected MTV to make money right away, but the entire Warner Amex cable operation, including cable stations and services like Nickelodeon, has been a money-loser from the start. Its losses of $46.6 million last year hurt Warner Communications, which was reeling from the disastrous performance of its Atari subsidiary.

"We're always reevaluating our financial state," says Pittman, and cost-cutting measures at MTV have been in place since early on. The most recent short-term plug in the money drain was the decision to charge new cable operators for carrying the service and the old ones when their contracts come up for renewal.

MTV's "success" has generated a slew of competitors, some of which already have larger audiences. Out of Atlanta, Ted Turner's SuperStation WTBS (with a potential cable audience of 27.6 million) has started *Night Tracks*, six hours of video late on Friday and Saturday nights, with music ranging from soul to rock to Top Forty. Also from Atlanta is the Video Music Channel, a budding network that programs a daily twelve-hour package of video clips (with a liberal sprinkling of black acts) for both cable and a full-time local UHF station. Vice-president Michael Greene sees the video package as "counterprogramming" to MTV.

USA Cable Networks' potential audience of over 21.5 million can watch ATI Video's weekend *Night Flight* (which hits its high point with rarely shown rock movies like *Rust Never Sleeps* and *Jimi Plays Berkeley*) and the weeknightly *Radio 1990*. ATI honcho Jeff Franklin also plans cable music video on other services besides USA Network; he's already introduced a syndicated show called *FM TV* on over-the-air television stations.

And now, with a potential audience of nearly the entire U.S., comes *Friday Night Videos*. Dick Ebersol, executive producer of *Saturday Night Live*, has taken over *SCTV*'s ninety-minute slot on NBC to show fifteen "of the very best" promo clips, along with some rock-oriented mini interviews. He will pay to air videos—around a thousand dollars per airing, except for "world premieres," which could earn considerably more. Ebersol thinks that the NBC exposure of the rock-video world will ultimately help MTV. But he hopes to draw the MTV audience for the duration of his show (and he does not deny that he would like to go longer than ninety minutes and more than one night).

Does MTV worry about Ebersol? Well, the channel refused to run a recent Robert Hazard video until it cut out a shot that showed a camera with the NBC peacock in plain view.

Still, the increased exposure of these promo clips will only make video an even more powerful force in the music business. And MTV, if its corporate parent hangs in there, remains the logical beneficiary of this bonanza. Only MTV, with its powerful rotation that saturates viewers with certain clips thirty-five times a week, can give the steady exposure that makes stars out of the likes of Adam Ant. And considering what we have seen of the video star-making machinery, the stars of the future will more likely be the superficial, easy-to-swallow Adam Ants than the enigmatic Bob Dylans.

As it is now, in the infancy of this revolution, MTV has become an obsession to the music industry. The video tail is wagging the musical dog.

Companies check out artists' "video potential" before signing them. In turn, the artists ask to receive front money for videos (though the standard deal is that a portion of the production money is considered an advance against royalties), sometimes even demanding that certain producers do their videos.

"They say, Get me the guy who did 'Allentown,' Get me the guy who did 'Billie Jean,'" moans Len Epand, who heads a brand-new division of the Polygram Group devoted solely to video production. "They don't understand that Russell Mulcahy charges more than $85,000 and Steve Barron costs $65,000 and up." The record companies have limited capitals and are reluctant to spend for videos when groups don't fit MTV's format. "We are going to make videos specifically for the MTV demographics," says Elektra-Asylum's Randy Edwards.

Concert promoters keep a close eye on MTV when they book artists. "If a band is on MTV, promoters are willing to pay more," says Ian Copeland of Frontier Booking International, beneficiary of a huge MTV promotion of this summer's Police tour. Retail outlets watch even more closely: "When I'm ordering new releases and the salesman says it's going to have a video on MTV, that definitely affects the quantity I order," says Record Bar's Norman Hunter.

The artists themselves are gung-ho on video. Even adamant hold-outs have come into the fold. Bob Seger, once a firm critic of video music, is now on MTV in heavy rotation. And despite David Bowie's objections to MTV's racist attitude, he's gone before the camera as an MTV pitchman. Other artists are starting to think MTV early on in the creative process. "I listen to things, and if I haven't seen the video, I almost can't get the full concept," says Patrick Simmons, a former Doobie Brother who's now soloing. Will he write with video in mind from now on? "Definitely. I think that's just the natural progression for music to take at this time. It's really exciting. I want my MTV."

All happy people, crooning the power of the MTV coalition. Happy that rock has wed itself to video, acquiescing to the burgeoning industry belief that success lies not in artistry, not in music, but in marketing a product to the proper psychographic. "It's the essence of America," says Bob Pittman, and once again, Bob Pittman is right on the money.

FROM 'RACE MUSIC' TO HEAVY METAL: A FIERY HISTORY OF PROTESTS[4]

Concerned that the nation's youth might be corrupted by "a wave of smut . . . breaking over the U.S. song trade," a powerful group condemns "salacious and suggestive songs," threatening to suppress offending but nevertheless popular numbers. A hit list of tunes that mock marriage and virginity, extol promiscuity and sexual prowess and flaunt the unconventional is published to

[4]Reprint of a magazine article by staff writer Steven Dougherty. *People Weekly.* 24:52+. S. 16, '85. Copyright © 1985 Time Inc. All rights reserved. Reprinted by permission of *People Weekly.*

bring public attention to the growing problem of pop pornography.

But it's not AC/DC that wrote *Lavender Cowboy*, and it's not Prince who composed *Dirty Lady* and *Keep Your Skirts Down, Mary Ann*. Nor is it Madonna who wrote *I'm a Virgin but I'm on the Verge*. No, these are among 147 recorded songs that the NBC radio network saw fit to ban in 1940. Cole Porter's *Love for Sale* was considered so "blue" that it could be broadcast only in instrumental form. Bessie Smith's bawdy classic about her "sugar bowl" sounded none too sweet to radio programmers, and Duke Ellington's *The Mooche* was considered so provocative that some blamed it for a national rise in incidents of rape. Such was the state of pop music before two active verbs—rock and roll—became a noun that meant something quite different to its fans than to those who would censor or sanitize it.

According to the *Rolling Stone Encyclopedia of Rock & Roll*, "the term [rock'n'roll] is a blues euphemism for sexual intercourse." Period. Attempts to present rock'n'roll to the public from the waist up, to package it in a plain brown wrapper, go back to its inception. Before Little Richard made your knees freeze and your liver quiver, before Elvis discovered the pelvis, rock'n'roll was called something else—"race music." As full of power, as liberating and as "sexually frank" as its offspring would prove to be, race music provoked little establishment ire for one obvious reason: Few white folk heard it.

It wasn't until race music "crossed over" to become rock'n'roll that the first real blacklash began, complete with blacklisting by radio, record burnings and rumblings from the fundamentalist right about white men who dared sing black—hillbilly cats like Elvis and Jerry Lee Lewis. To quell protests and expand markets, white-owned record companies and radio broadcasters encouraged white artists like Pat Boone to "cover"—and cleanse—black records. One of many examples: Hank Ballard and the Midnighters' risqué classic, *Work With Me, Annie*, claims Frank Zappa, became Georgia Gibbs' *Dance With Me, Henry*. That song, Zappa points out, featured the same melody and chord changes but different words.

Aside from such early rock purists as disc jockey Alan Freed, who refused to play the white versions, rock's elder defenders were few. "Dirty boogying" teens were evicted from dance parties everywhere. Asbury Park, the New Jersey coastal town that

would later gain fame as the artistic home turf of Bruce Springsteen, was one of the American cities that passed legislation ban-
ning rock'n'roll concerts and dances in civic buildings. On Sept.
9, 1956, when the *Ed Sullivan Show* aired Elvis from the waist up
only, the *New York Times* nevertheless found the performance
"filthy." To such critics Elvis responded: "They all think I'm a sex
maniac. They're just frustrated old types anyway. I'm just
normal."

Except for sporadic record burnings in the Deep South and
persistent attempts to have the Kingsmen's *Louie Louie* formally
banned from the radio (after repeated listenings, members of the
Federal Communications Commission concluded that the song
could not corrupt youth since not a word was decipherable), rock
composers were pretty much left alone until the mid-'60s, when
political protest and drug references became the new irritants of
choice.

In 1970, after Vice President Spiro Agnew said in a speech
that rock music was being used to brainwash America's children
into using drugs, a crusade was launched to expose drug imagery
in rock songs. Agnew's campaign brought some unusual charac-
ters out of the woodwork. Speaking at the Movement to Restore
Decency rally in Minneapolis in 1970, one Joseph R. Crow alerted
the crowd to his theory that most rock musicians are "part of a
Communist movement to incite revolution throughout the
world."

Seven years later, the censorious Agnew found an unlikely
ally in the Rev. Jesse Jackson. Songs like *Shake Your Booty, Let's
Make a Baby* and *I Want To Do Something Freaky to You*, Jackson
said, contain "suggestive lyrics" that promote promiscuity and
drug use. Jackson's comments were prompted by the public's fas-
cination with disco's "sex rock"; Donna Summer's *Love to Love You
Baby*, for example, was described at the time as a "marathon of
22 orgasms." In 1975 one interested party, the Rev. Charlie
Boykin of Tallahassee, Fla., set fire to thousands of dollars' worth
of rock records, citing a local poll that said 984 of 1,000 unwed
mothers interviewed got pregnant while listening to pop songs.

By the early '80s, inspired by the demonic doings of such
heavy metal groups as Led Zeppelin and Black Sabbath, the focus
of numerous cleanup drives had already zeroed in on another
problem area—satanic violence. Thus, when a 25-year-old grocery store employee named Art Diaz heard his wife describe a

church seminar on the influence of Satan and devil-worship in rock music, he was moved to action. Assembling a group of teenagers from the local First Assembly of God Church in Des Moines in October 1980, Diaz and his charges burned 30 album covers after breaking their vinyl contents. Among those fried were works by the Beatles, Peter Frampton and sitarist Ravi Shankar. Diaz said he also threw in a tape of the sound track from the movie *Grease*.

The next spring, nightclub owner Jeff Jochims of Carroll, Iowa suddenly announced he was going to close his mud wrestling/disco club and atone for past sins by setting afire $2,000 worth of albums that he felt encouraged illicit sex and drug abuse. Two hundred and fifty miles away in Keokuk, a church group spent a Sunday afternoon burning albums they believed "subliminally influenced" young people. The subversive musicians included Perry Como, the Carpenters and John Denver.

THE PUNK MEETS THE GODMOTHER[5]

London, April 1977

• *It took a bit of courage to start this article, as I have said precisely nothing to the press (other than through lyrics) for close to two years. Today, reading it through, there is much I am tempted to add or expand on. There is a strong temptation to bring everything up to date, but then the success of the Who's last tour did that. The future, of course, is an open book.*

The sections in italics are merely pieces of my writing from about November 1973 to November 1975, the months covered in the article. I often sit at a typewriter and knock-out stream-of-consciousness stuff. It not only helps clear the head but often brings forth ideas for songs. These were written on scraps of paper at dead of night, at the lunch table with the kids on my lap, in hotel rooms while filming or performing. They were never meant to be published, so they are somewhat obscure, but they are minimally edited and therefore revelatory of my state of mind and degree of intoxicated desperation.

    [5]Reprint of a magazine article by songwriter and guitarist Pete Townshend. From *Rolling Stone*. p54+. N. 17, '77. By Straight Arrow Publishers, Inc. © 1977. All rights reserved. Reprinted by Permission.

I used to be highly talkative with the rock press and have missed my contact with writers. Silence, however, is habit-forming, and I am glad to be able to look back objectively to such an emotional period of my life with the band and try to say it right. What I never expected was such sympathy and understanding from writers who I continually put off when they asked for interviews or even just a chat. I have lost contact with many journalist friends because I have been scared to speak. This article helps bring things up-to-date. Perhaps in the future I can get used to working jaws again, instead of my fingers—fingers that would be better occupied playing guitars or tickling children.

February 1st, 1977. Today I received a letter from a neighbor. She says I must forgive her for ignoring me, but it's because of her religion. She knows I have a crush on her. I'm not sure who she is, but I might well have a crush on her if I did; she wrote a letter to my wife saying the same thing. Irritating.

It's now 2:30 in the morning, and I can't get to sleep. My crush on my neighbor has become so strong that it will only be satisfied when I have thrilled to the delight of actually crushing her. I sometimes wonder where this piece of my destiny was forged: anyone can sum me up at a glance, my life is on sale. All I know is that it sometimes hurts to be exposed, and to be unable to retaliate without feeding the haggling customers.

Yesterday was Meher Baba's "Amartithi." Followers of this great Master (to whom I remain committed) celebrate the anniversary of his passing in 1969. In the afternoon, I saw a film of his entombment and felt a most powerful feeling of his presence throughout the day. It is incredible to me—as I'm sure it is to many witnesses of my day-to-day behavior—that I still feel so moved by Meher Baba's words, photographs and films. After following him for nearly nine years, I have fallen deeply into the rhythm of focusing all my reflections on life through a lens formed of experience I have had under his spiritual umbrella.

That letter and the film: as extremes, they seem to indicate the incredible paradoxes and conflicts that surround me. The most amazing thing of all is that my head has surfaced, some distance from the shoreline of past paranoia, in an ocean of immeasurable possibilities. I feel strong and secure and, for the first time, able to talk about the Who (or at least the Who through my eyes) back in '74–'75.

If I try to imagine where my head was two years ago, it's a strange vision. Paranoia does not adequately describe my feelings, though I suppose all of the Who were to a degree paranoid toward one another. But my trouble was also manifestly spiritual. I felt I had let myself down morally and artistically; I felt quite genuinely to be a hypocrite. I complained a lot about things that I felt I was doing from the goodness of my heart but wasn't receiving enough attention for: to pick only one example from many, helping Eric Clapton. I spent a tremendous amount of time with him during his heroin cure, and earned his love as a result. What originally happened was that I'd been going down to see him, because I figured that if people started to go and see him, he might come out of his habit. I knew him well from the Hendrix days, of course, and I enjoy his company. Also, Alice, the woman he was living with, and I really hit it off. Then David Harlech, her father, spoke to me. He said that Eric wanted to do a concert if I would run it. I felt I had no choice but to agree, and it was instrumental in getting him to John and Meg Patterson, whose acupuncture cure did eventually rid Eric of his addiction. But my wife measured it all against time spent with her, fairly minimal at the best of times, and *very* minimal during this period (around November 1973). There is no point pretending that it is possible to help bring a man off heroin while you're doing a nine-to-five office job. "Tea and meet the wife" don't mix with three a.m. phone calls and Rainbow reunion rehearsals that actually *start* at six in the morning!

At the same time, a confrontation with Roger Daltrey was building. While working with Eric, I was also writing and recording *Quadrophenia*. Kit Lambert had helped a certain amount while I was writing, and had promised to produce the album. He didn't make out very well, and argued with Daltrey. I felt let down and took over, despite the fact that I had more than enough on my plate.

When the album was completed, it took only a few days for Roger to express his disgust at the result. I had spent my summer vacation mixing it, and he had popped in once to hear mixes, making a couple of negative comments about the sound but seeming quite keen to let me "have my head," as it were, in production. Fundamentally, I had taken on too much, as always, and couldn't handle the strain when things went wrong and people blamed me.

I felt I was perfectly entitled to gamble and lose, as no one else seemed prepared to, either with *Quadrophenia* or even the Who's career.

So, I felt angry at Roger for not realizing how much work I had done on the album—apart from writing it—and angry that he dismissed my production as garbage. It's hard to explain, because I don't feel these things anymore. I genuinely feel I was the one who was in the wrong. But it contributed a lot to what happened later.

• *I was in one of those shallow sleeps when dreams are clear as day, but each scene in the unfolding reverie is also strangely dark. I gazed at an ocean scene, thinking to myself, "I am dreaming. I control my movements through my sleeping adventures."*

In a dream within a dream, I awoke for a minute. I looked around the room. Everything was as it should be: the chair in its usual place, with my previous day's clothing strewn over the back. The dead television gazed at me quietly; the window blind was pulled right down, the bathroom light still on, towels on the floor damp and tangled.

I closed my eyes and became aware of a strange feeling. Not of an impending nightmare or even the experience of unease, though the whole scene seemed set for troubling vision. On the contrary, a sense of elation came over me. I snuggled my weary head into my pillow like a child and smiled at the strong buzz of contentment that flooded my mind.

At that moment, I heard something distant that seemed to reflect my almost orgasmic feelings of pleasure. Years before, I had experimented with a tape recording of dozens and dozens of piano performances, sweeping and glittering over the entire chromatic scale. I then mixed them all together as one and the result was an almost unidentifiable sound, but of great beauty and mystery. A sound like waves crashing, or distant wind over a summit, but musical. In fact, on occasion a glimpse of detail within the deluge manifested, and piano could be clearly heard.

This new, remote sound I heard in my dream had similarities to my experimental work. It sounded like a breath being gently sighed away, but the listener's ear seemed inside the mouth of a lion. Listen to your own breath. Breathe out in a quiet place and hear the beauty and complexity of the sound. The slightest change in the shape of your mouth chamber, the tiniest movement of your lips, and the breath becomes a song or a word. A thousand harmonics are thrown up like glittering reflections on the surface of a sunlit bay. In the mystic's "Om" is contained every sound, and every sound within a sound. Every ingredient that contributes to the source of the primordial desire to even make a sound is contained in that one word.

So this is the train of thought I was taking in my dream. I was still aware that I was asleep, but it seemed unimportant. The new sound grew louder, began to come closer. Then the miracle surpassed itself, the beauty of the sound became transcendentally glorious. Its superficial simplicity only disguised a secret ingredient that, I felt, must in itself contain all things.

This roaring, singing, cascading sound threw me into an ecstasy that almost defied description. But while swooning under its import and unparalleled attractiveness, I still had the presence of mind—perhaps because I am a musician—to try to analyze and discover what this incredible music was. If I could only break down this sound I could remake it for the whole world to hear. I could make a reality of this outer limit of my unleashed and unfettered musical imagination: glorious, celestial music of only dreams.

I began to listen more carefully, trying to ignore the hyperbolic sweetness of the sound—almost like a starving man trying to eat a piece of cheese and at the same time compose a thesis on the relative distinction between, say, double Gloucester and caerphilly.

Recklessly, I plunged deeply into the music. As I became submerged, it became slightly more coarse; it was, indeed, like diving into the sea. The feeling of the sharp, cool water is always a shock when one has spent an hour gazing languidly at the sunny surface of the waves. I could still hear the rippling and soaring of the incomparable sigh, and I was now in it, of it. I delved even more deeply into the secret. What was the essential ingredient of this music? What was its fundamental element?

For a few minutes, I was lost in my search. I forgot to listen quite so intently and began turning over in my mind the various possibilities and alternatives. Was it a million pianos? Perhaps the sound of a heavenly choir?

That was it! The heart of this sound was the human voice: there could be no question. I plunged headlong, further into the chasm of this incorporal symphony. As I thrust inward, it was apparently simplifying.

Then, in a second, the whole world seemed to turn inside out. My skin crawled as I recognized the unit elements of this superficially wonderful noise. I could not believe what I heard. As I tore myself away, I felt I was leaving sections of my self behind, caught up in the cacophonous dirge. I tried to wake myself, but only succeeded in breaking through a superficial level—no longer a dream within a dream, merely a nightmare. A game, a ghastly trick perpetrated on me by my own mind. A vitiated and *distorted ploy of my ego to stunt my trust in nature's beauty, kill my appetite for the constant, for the One within the many, the many within the One.*

For the sound that I was hearing was the Niagran roar of a billion humans screaming.

Now I really awoke. Ironically, the room looked just as it had in the dream. Nothing had changed. My body was soaking wet; sweat seeped from every pore. Fever lay under the surface of my skin like a disease. I leapt from my bed, clutching a small bead on a string that I knew had been touched by my Master, and prayed for protection. I felt enough comfort to clear my head and allow me to draw a conclusion. I now know that of all things on earth, nothing is so inherently evil, so contemptuous, so vile, so conniving, so worthless . . . as my own imagination.

Quadrophenia (the Who's last major album with a contrived theme, released in 1973) tried to describe the utopian secrets of the eternal youth of each Who member. We get our life extensions from our audiences. However far down we go as individuals, there will always be rent to pay, so always an audience. When there's an audience, there's salvation. Mixed up in *Quadrophenia* was a study of the divine desperation that is at the root of every punk's scream for blood and vengeance.

I can elaborate. It is really fantastic conceit on the part of the Establishment to imagine that any particular fragment of society is ever the true subject of a rock & roll song. Even in the famous, folk-oriented, political complaining songs of the very early Sixties, a thread of upward groping for truth came through strongly. The definition of rock & roll lies here for me. If it screams for truth rather than help, if it commits itself with a courage it can't be sure it really has, if it stands up and admits something is wrong but doesn't insist on blood, then it's rock & roll.

We shed our own blood. We don't need to shed anyone else's.

When I sit and listen to "The Punk Meets the Godfather" on *Quadrophenia*, I come closer to defining my state three years ago. I was the Godfather. (When I met two of the Sex Pistols recently, I was in an appropriately raging, explosive mood, but I recognized their hungry, triumph-pursuant expressions and began to preach.)

In '73 and '74, I was the aging daddy of punk rock. I was bearing a standard I could barely hold up anymore. My cheeks were stuffed, not with cotton wool in the Brando-Mafioso image, but with the scores of uppers I had taken with a sneer and failed to swallow.

On the Who's tour of the U.S. and Canada in the fall of '76 a lot of things came to a "glorious" head in Toronto, the last show of the tour. The road crew threw a party for us, and it was the first party I had been to for at least five years which meant anything to me. I don't go to a lot of parties, but I'm glad that I made this one. I suddenly realized that behind every Who show are people who care as much as, or more than, we do. Talking to the individuals who help get the show together enabled me to remember that audiences care, too.

When I sit in an audience, one of the things that makes it enjoyable is the energy I spent *willing* it to be the best thing I have ever seen. I get to see some great concerts that way. Ask any Who fan if they care how well we are playing on any single date. The Who don't count as much as people might imagine, but as performers their response to the audience's energy is vital.

So two years ago when I felt down, when I felt empty, tired and defeated, the audience of Who freaks carried on regardless. At the time I was very bitter about this. I remember our concerts at Madison Square Garden, having come out of total seclusion in my studio after preparing mind-bending and complex tracks for the *Tommy* film. When my drunken legs gave way under me, as I tried to do a basic cliché leap and shuffle, a few loving fans got up a chant. "Jump! Jump! Jump!" Brings tears to your eyes, doesn't it? It did mine anyway. Such loyalty!

• *This man had consumed time in a way that only God Himself could ever hold a candle to, but had he learned anything? He belongs to God, as we all do. Deny that He is, then, God's folly and what do you do? You refute God Himself.*

That argument is for cozy firesides. No, this was God's work. The devil is, after all, only a figment of God's imagination. And so this remarkable fool believed himself to be a figment of a figment. A dream within a dream. He believed he had an imagination that could not be shaken by the actual imagination that brought forth his very own being!

Such impudence.

Such unwitting humor.

Life could easily continue the provision of sideshows in this one's circus. Perhaps his endless dream could be shattered this time.

Maybe this little man's time had really come.

The general rule of the day in show business was, "When in or out of trouble—drink," so I drank some more. Drinking around the Who is the greatest thing gutter-level life can offer. The bawdiness of the humor, the sheer decadence of the amount put away, the incredible emotional release of violent outbursts against innocent hotel-room sofas; all these count to get a body through a lot of trouble. But at the end of the orgy, the real cancer still lies untackled deep in the heart.

When the Who were recording *The Who by Numbers*, Keith's courageous attempts to head off his alcoholism moved me to stop drinking too. I stopped overnight. The results were interesting. My hair started to fall out. Another remarkable side effect was that I carried on drinking without my knowledge. This story can only carry credence if we are to believe the observations of the people around us when we were recording; they were probably twice as drunk as I. Apparently, at the end of one session which I had gotten through by pulling incessantly at a total of about twenty cans of Coke, I wished everyone good night, walked up to a makeshift bar and drank a bottle of vodka. I just don't remember doing that.

I got very scared by memory blackouts, as scared as I had ever been on bad LSD trips eight years before. Once in July 1974—just after the *Tommy* filming—I sort of "came to" in the back of my own car. Keith and John were with me (we were probably going to a club), but although I knew who they were, I didn't recognize either my car or my driver, who had been working for me for about two months. The shock that hit me as the pieces fell into place was even more frightening than the black holes in my head as the memory lapses began. Eight drug-free years and still this mental demise.

On another occasion, at the "thank you" concert we gave in Portsmouth, England, for the extras in the *Tommy* film, I signed several managerial and recording contracts in a complete fog. The only event I remember is quietly screaming for help deep inside, as I asked John Entwistle if it had ever happened to him. (The fact that I'd signed the contracts didn't come home to me until we were actually in the middle of a legal rangle some months later.)

Tommy has become rock's "Pirates of Penzance" in only ten years of exposure to the public, through the Who's performances onstage, their original album, Lou Reizner's album with the London Symphony Orchestra, Ken Russell's film, the ballet of the Royal Canadian Ballet and dozens of minor exploitations such as "Electric Tommy," the music played on synthesizer, and "Marching Tommy," the music scored for college brass bands.

The above, in a simple way, illustrates how as a rock composer and performer I was dragged into the world of light entertainment and into the world of high finance. The Who's original *Tommy* album sold very well indeed in comparison to their early record sales, and as a result the band was baled out of terrific debt and given a new lease on life in many ways. As for the reference to light entertainment: *Tommy* was never ever really meant to be as "heavy" as, say, "My Generation." We joked as a group about *Tommy* being true opera, which it isn't, but the Who's audience, and many of the rock press took it very seriously indeed. It was this seriousness that turned *Tommy* into light entertainment.

Many Who fans feel the *Tommy* film is not what the Who is about, or even what *Tommy* is about. In truth, it is exactly what it is about. It is the prime example of rock & roll throwing off its three-chord musical structure, discarding its attachment to the three-minute single, openly taking on the unfashionable questions about spirituality and religion and yet hanging grimly on to the old ways at the same time.

I enjoyed doing the *Tommy* film. I liked the opportunity to re-work some of the music, and bring it up to date soundwise, and I genuinely admired and respected Ken Russell, who is stimulating company but an obsessive worker. Being sympathetic to that strange condition. I suppose I allowed myself to work beyond my capabilities.

We spent about six weeks preparing the tracks before shooting began in April 1974. During the second week of the actual filming, I declared to Bill Curbishly, our new manager, that I would never work on the road with the Who again. I think I might even have said that I felt the Who was finished.

I was mixed up by my two professions: as writer and musical director on the film, and as performer with the Who. I think I perhaps blamed the Who's live work for bringing me to such an emotional abyss. In retrospect, I know that it is only from the Who's live concerts that I get energy freely for doing practically nothing. I play guitar, I jump and dance, and come off stronger than when I went on. Walking offstage after a Who concert, we each feel like superhumans. It's easy to mistake this very genuine and natural energy high for innate stamina of some God-given talent for an endless adrenalin supply.

After my total downward spiral during the filming of *Tommy*, and after living with the desperate fear of further humiliation of the Madison Square Garden variety, I did a few interviews with the London-based rock press. My final undoing was to see among them a face I knew and to imagine that it belonged to someone who cared about me more as a person than as a rock performer. I should never have expected that.

Blaming the group, I blurted out my fears, my depressions and woe to a couple of writers whose sympathies were, to put it mildly, a little to the left wing of rock journalism. When they appeared in print, the results were catastrophic. Roger was understandably outraged, and retaliated to my abject misery in his own interviews published a few weeks later. "I knocked Townshend out with one punch." I think I was already dead before it connected.

I feel now as though we were both, to an extent, manipulated by a skillful and opportunistic reporting chain, that the derision handed out to me by Roger for my weakness and indulgence did me a lot of good. It hurt me at the time, but when you're so far down, so the saying goes, the gutter looks up. I had, after all, been derisive of Roger in print many times.

Roger went to work on another Ken Russell film, *Lisztomania*, which I managed to avoid. I got my head down to try to write a bit for the coming album (*The Who by Numbers*) and came up with some reality tinged with bitterness. It was hard for me to admit what I knew as I was composing: that what was happening to me was an exorcism. Suicide notes tend to flush out the trouble felt by the potential ledge jumpers. But once the truth is out, there's no need to leap.

I also felt curiously mixed up about my state of mind. "Slip Kid" came across as a warning to young kids getting into music that it would hurt them—it was almost parental in its assumed wisdom. "Blue, Red and Gray" was a ukelele ditty with John Entwistle adding brass band to the misty middle distance. It was about nothing at all; it reminded me of an old *Smiley Smile* Beach Boys number. "A Hand or a Face" was cynical and tried to cut down the growing dependence I had on mysticism and psychic phenomena. All the songs were different, some more aggressive than others, but they were all somehow negative in direction. I felt empty.

Recording the album seemed to take me nowhere. Roger was angry with the world at the time. Keith seemed as impetuous as ever, on the wagon one minute, off it the next. John was obviously gathering strength throughout the whole period; the great thing about it was that he seemed to know we were going to need him more than ever before in the coming year.

Glyn Johns, who was producing the album, was going through the most fantastic traumas at home with his marriage. I felt partly responsible because the Who recording schedule had, as usual, dragged on and on, sweeping all individuals and their needs aside. Glyn worked harder on *The Who by Numbers* than I've ever seen him. He had to, not because the tracks were weak or the music poor (though I'll admit it's not a definitive Who album), but because the group was so useless. We played cricket between takes or went to the pub. I personally had never done that before. I felt detached from my own songs, from the whole record; though I did discover some terrific sportsmen in our road crew.

After we finished recording in August 1975, we had a month off. I decided to try to get some spiritual energy from friends in the U.S.A. For a few years, I had toyed with the idea of opening a London house dedicated to Meher Baba. In the eight years I had followed him, I had donated only coppers to foundations set up around the world to carry out the Master's wishes and decided it was about time I put myself on the line. The Who had set up a strong charitable trust of its own which appeased, to an extent, the feeling I had that Meher Baba would rather have seen me give to the poor than to the establishment of yet another so-called "spiritual center."

My family (particularly of course my wife, who as a matter of personal policy tries to avoid the aspects of the music world that I still find exciting) had suffered a lot from my pathetic behavior of the previous year, but they would naturally be by my side on any trip other than Who tours. So they came with me, or rather I went with them, to Myrtle Beach, South Carolina, where Meher Baba had set up a retreat during the Fifties. I intended to travel on after a couple of weeks to spend a full month living under the wing of Murshida Duce in California. Murshida Duce is the appointed head of the Sufi movement in the States, as reoriented under Meher Baba's directives. She is used to recognizing and helping her initiates with emotional problems and had invited me to come to be with her and her family when she had visited England in October '74.

I was genuinely unprepared for the unfolding that transpired in that six weeks. My mind was clouded with the idea of trying to run a "center" for Avatar Meher Baba; with the difficulties I would have trying to deal with people's whims and complaints; but most of all, with the hypocrisy of trying to do such a contentiously idealistic thing while enjoying the kind of life I had been living.

• *I spent the last three days of March talking about punk rock with Chris Stamp. I'm sure I invented it, and yet it's left me behind. If anything was ever a refutation of time, my constant self-inflicted adolescence must be.*

Chris told me the punk crowds banged their heads through ceilings, swore at one another, and if a fight broke out (though "breaking out" is hardly the term to use in this context), one became the aggressor, one the victim. The crowd was one, the fighters played out roles.

Damage, damage, damage. It's a great way to shake society's value system. It makes mothers disown their children. It makes schoolteachers puke.

High-rise blocks and slums in Glasgow—I don't need to have lived in them to know the facts. I see the faces beaming up at me as I destroy my £500 guitar. Why should they, poor bastards, dig that? They enjoy the destruction because they despise phony values; the heavy price on the scrap of tin called a musical instrument. It is so far beyond their reach it might as well not exist.

The crucifixion is what these people stand for. They humiliate themselves and their peers, and care nothing for any accolade. These stars are true stars; they are part of an audience of stars.

> *And on the dance floor broken glass,*
> *The bloody faces slowly pass,*
> *The numbered seats in empty rows;*
> *It all belongs to me you know*

Where am I in space that I should care so much about the lonely souls in tiny square bedrooms a hundred feet up in air in cities all over the world?

I am with them. I want nothing more than to go with them to their desperate hell, because that loneliness they suffer is soon to be over. Deep inside, they know.

*I prayed for it, and yet it's too late for me to truly participate. I feel
like an engineer.*

Just let me . . . watch.

Paris: George V Hôtel, May 1975.

• *I came to in a kind of trance. The woman with me is my wife; she is
quite uniquely beautiful. Her profile is serene and encouraging. I look
down at myself and I'm dressed rather peculiarly. My face is hairless and
my jacket waisted with a 15-inch inverted pleat at the back. My shoes are
scratched and worn. My collar feels too tight. I glance in the mirror as
we walk to the restaurant. Is that the so-called "me"?*

*Children? Where are the children? I was sure that I would have beau-
tiful, sparkling children. Where are they?*

*We walk into the long, elegant room and wait to be seated. The head-
waiter acknowledges our hand gestures in French. It is Paris.*

*The woman is smiling with an exhilarated jubilance to fit a queen.
I glance along the room at nearby tables. They are all staring at her, en-
tranced. The head waiter suggests we drink Beaujolais Villages, slightly
chilled. It costs nothing—there are wines on the menu that cost $100—but
he suggests this simple fare. When it is delivered, we understand. The
warmth of perfection that accompanies such instants is unmeasurable.
The way the silken cloth clings to her body, revealing not only the perfection of her form, but also the eccentricities: the faults (if it is possible to
call them that).*

*We eat, the food is superb; why is everything so right? Is Paris really
a dream? In our room, the blinds are wound down, the sparkling white
sheets revealed in a triangle.*

*How does this fit in? I remember dingy dance halls, fish and chips
and little cheap cars that break down miles from home.*

*I stare into the future. Nothing that I have ever dreamed of has failed
me. So I stare knowing that what I see will be. It's not clairvoyance so
much as fatal determination, and yet I know that one day my luck must
inevitably run out.*

What am I doing with this superb woman? What am I doing?

In early August, before I left England, I had written Roger
a note, telling him that I felt there had been a lot of unnecessary
strife between us, and that I hoped I could earn his respect again.
From New York on the first leg of our trip to Carolina, I wrote
to him again (he was on the road promoting his new album, *Ride
a Rock Horse*). I told him I would support him in whatever he did.
I felt it a strange thing to say.

I had always been the helmsman of the Who, Roger—and Keith, John and our management as well—always had plenty to say in the group's affairs. But because I wrote the majority of songs, they were inexorably tied up in my feelings, emotions and directions. I took the band over when they asked me to write for them in 1964 in order to pass the Decca audition, and used them as a mouthpiece, hitting out at anyone who tried to have a say in what the group said (mainly Roger) and then grumbling when they didn't appreciate my dictatorship. Roger often sang songs I'd written that he didn't care for with complete commitment, and I took him for granted. I said what I wanted to say, often ignoring or being terribly patronizing about the rest of the group's suggestions, then sulked when they didn't worship me for making life financially viable. (Kit Lambert went through the same process; he did great work for the Who, not realizing that we were satisfied that he should be thanked, credited and presumably made to feel quite happy by his royalty check each month.)

In New York, a good friend of mine gave me some advice. I tried to explain that I felt the problems in the Who were mainly about me and Roger, not the myriad business problems that seemed so manifestly cancerous. I was counseled quite simply: "Let Roger win."

The statement isn't as cruel or flippant as it sounds. This person knew the Who and its history and cared about all of us deeply. The advice meant that I should demonstrate to Roger that my letters were sincere by not hanging on to past grievances or differences. Most of all, I should bow to the changing status quo within the group, created by the fans' new identification with Roger as front man, rather than with me as its mouthpiece.

John and Keith are probably chewing my photo right now. I know what always irritates them most is when a journalist describes them as "Pete Townshend's puppets!" If the Who has been a tyranny in the past, it's been ruled by a runaway horse. Roger has always seen the group in a more objective light than I; as things stand today, the balance within the group as a result of his more active role in its creative direction has brought me closer than ever to Roger and Keith and John as well.

Were it not for the recently resolved legal dispute between the Who and its old management team—Kit Lambert and Chris Stamp—I would probably ramble on about it all at great length. Let it just be said, perhaps because I am a Taurus, perhaps be-

cause I am sentimental, that I had resisted Roger for many years
in his justifiable revolution against our managers. That had never
helped our relationship one iota. (Incidentally, the group's subsequent split with Pete Rudge's New York–based Sir Productions
was an amicable one, but again Rudge and I found time to cry in
our beer over lost partnerships. We had often shared a cell after
the frequent Who hotel debacles.) As for Kit and Chris, my feelings now can be summed up concisely: I miss them.

Against this backdrop of good intentions, I set off in August
1975 to Myrtle Beach. As our party (my wife, my two little daughters and a few friends who traveled with us) crossed the threshold
onto Meher Baba's home ground, we were all staggered by the
impact of the love that literally filled the air.

Despite the strength I felt growing within me, I think I can
speak for our whole party when I say I felt exhausted by Myrtle
Beach. God's endlessly present love isn't to be taken lightly. It's
great to be forgiven, but it hurts to admit you were wrong in the
first place. I realized that I would not be reaping such fantastic
emotional and mental rewards had I not been in pretty bad shape;
a condition for which I had no one to blame but myself.

When you hold out an empty cup to God and demand that He
fill it with wine, He fills it faster than you can ever drink. Then
you know that the fault is your own incapacity to receive His infinite love, rather than His capacity to give it. I loosely quote Hafiz
here, of course, but this is what I felt was happening. Even my
youngest daughter, Aminta, three years old, became starry-eyed
with the atmosphere that poured from the trees. I woudn't say
that the warm reception given us by the residents of the Myrtle
Beach retreat was not enjoyed and appreciated, but it paled in significance when compared to the welcome we felt in the buzzing
dragonflies, the sound of the ocean and the massaging humidity
of the warm afternoon.

We spent an unbelievable ten days. I talked to the older devotees of Meher Baba about my plans for a new place in London and
they were naturally encouraging. The sun shone, the children enjoyed themselves, we relaxed and relished rejuvenation at the
Master's command. The fears I had that I would not be strong
enough to see through the imminent testing rehearsals and tour
with the Who receded.

We traveled then to California.

• *I look out through your bloodshot eyes and I ask you, does this really matter? I am here, and I want constantly as your hair falls over the type-writer keys."*

I don't want to die . . . !

"Death is not at all what I expect. I want surrender, surely that is simple enough."

I am suffocating in your love . . . help me somebody! I am drowning!

"They say that to drown in the depths is really to ascend."

Beloved God, why do you sometimes bring me close to tears?

"Because I am your own heart, you might well be bored with me. I am you. And have known, and lived, and died with you . . . for a billion years."

In California, we were well looked after, taken into the bosom of the Sufi family there, provided with a furnished house, picnics, swimming pool, outings to state parks, camping trips to the Sierras and all kinds of straight-laced relaxation.

You are probably as mystified as I am as to where the spiritually beneficial work was being done in this kind of program, but spirit was what was needed, and spirit was what I got, even if it didn't fit preconceived notions.

Murshida Duce is a remarkable woman. She heads a group of about 300 initiates, all committed to total honesty and respect for her authority. She has Meher Baba's sanction as the legitimate Murshid along with "in line" decree from her own deceased Murshid, Murshida Martin. Murshida Martin herself took over under the instructions of the famous Inayat Khan, a spiritual teacher and master musician whose books on Sufism present a poetic system for modern life.

"Sufism Reoriented" today focuses its initiates on developing their devotion to Meher Baba. Meher Baba gave an explicit charter to Murshida Duce and it is under the limitations of this charter that she works today. I am not a Sufi initiate, but her spontaneous help in my life has always touched me. I felt it extraordinary that she was clearly comfortable with me. She is a rather grand lady in late years, accustomed in her own youth to formal dinners and cocktail parties for her husband's work as an oil man in the Forties and Fifties. In fact, she is not so easily pigeonholed.

On arrival in California, I went for a talk with her, to gossip, to bring her up-to-date on events at home, to ask her advice about the color of the walls at the newly planned Baba house in London. Instead, to my amazement, I sat and poured out my very soul. I couldn't for a second have anticipated this happening. She sat and listened as I told her every grisly detail; the paranoia, the drunken orgies, the financial chaos, the indulgent self-analysis (continued herein, I'm afraid) and, of course, the dreamy hopes for the future.

Without batting an eyelid she listened to stuff that was making me recoil myself, then went on to talk a little about her own youth, her life with her husband, the trouble some of her students were having at the time. In short, she got me right in perspective.

At the end of this month with her, we packed our bags, said our farewells and headed home, my wife and the kids to school, me to rehearsals with the band. Keith later told me I walked into the rehearsal hall smiling; he related this because he had found it remarkable. Something positive had happened to me.

Back in England, I got hold of a building for the London Meher Baba house and one morning, early, sat thinking about the past year. I thought about the incredibly circuitous route I had taken to bring me to that point in October 1975, a new British Who tour ahead of us. I got to where I ended up. Having taken energy, freely given, from just about every source I could lay my hands on, being strong again and feeling fairly certain that I could now rock & roll right into my grave, I decided that I could dare to ask for just one more directive.

I raised my eyes to the heavens, my future Meher Baba house looming up as a great potential encroachment on my time with band, and asked the old man: "What conclusions do I draw from all this, Baba? Where do I put this love you've given me?"

The answer came out of the sky, in a voice that, to me, was audible in a fantastic sense: *"Keep playing the guitar with the Who until further notice."*

• *Where am I and what am I? I kneel at the foot of a picture of my Master, I plead forgiveness, but in dreams I gloat. The superb and beautiful creatures that have lain at my feet. What am I? I look in the mirror and don't see much. Am I purely a fraud? Fall in, all you cynics, but how about your own admirers?*

The people I observe fall at my feet, but why?

I think I know. The ego floods away from me like the crutch snatched from a cripple. But the feeling is not bad: they love me for what I could be, not for what I am.

When I screamed for God to smash me down, I didn't expect for a minute that he really would.

June 20th, 1977.

• *The editors have asked what I feel precipitated this crisis. Caring too much? Is it possible? I have read that stars and punk people take themselves too seriously. I am both star and punk, therefore I take myself so seriously that I actually believe I matter to the world. I matter firstly to my family, then to the group and its fans, then to the few who have the conviction that Meher Baba is the True Avatar. In that order. I get serious when Pete Townshend disrupts this scheme of priorities as an individual; when his neuroses and paranoia break up the matter-of-fact interpretation of the scheme's direction.*

Keith Moon once sat in a hotel bed in Boston after dying on the stage in front of 10,000 or so kids, and said, quite simply, "I've let you down." Not, "I've let the Who down," not "I've let down the people." He'd let us down.

My crisis was caused by no one and nothing. It cost me nothing; it gives me everything. It was never precipitated because precipitation is a slow process. Rock & roll is fast. There was no waiting for time to take its course, or for me to weigh up whether I was doing right or wrong. Rock & roll always tries to do right. Rock & roll always aims high and offers itself up as the tinderwood to the fire that will burn away the crap in this world. Rock & roll uses up people, music and talent, even genius, like balsa in a roaring inferno. The fire burns brightly even when the fuel supply gets low, because there is always someone ready to give everything in a last-ditch attempt to gain fame. The right is that it tries, the wrong is that it often fails.

My crisis was simply that I felt I was failing rock & roll. And for me this was a crime. For in doing this, I was failing friends and family, history, the future and, most important of all, I was failing God. No one less could have invented this sublime music.

BIBLIOGRAPHY

An asterisk (*) preceding a reference indicates that the article or part of it has been reprinted in this book.

BOOKS AND PAMPHLETS

Anscombe, Isabelle, Bayley, Roberta and Blair, Dike. Punk. Urizen Books, '78.

Arredondo, Mike, Kulakofsky, Rob and Robert, Gary. Hardcore rock 'n' roll. IN3D. '84.

Baker, Glenn A. and Coupe, Stuart. The new music. Harmony Books. '81. (rev. ed.)

Baker, Glenn A. and Coupe, Stuart. The new rock 'n' roll. Omnibus Press. '83.

Bane, Michael. The outlaws: revolution in country music. Doubleday. '78.

Bangs, Lester. Blondie. Omnibus Press. '80.

Bangs, Lester and Nelson, Paul. Rod Stewart. Delilah Communications. '81.

Barnes, Richard. The Who: maximum R q B. St. Martin's Press. '82.

Barrett, Leonard Emanuel. The Rastafarians: the dreadlocks of Jamaica. Heinemann Educational. '77.

Belsito, Peter and Davis, Bob. Hardcore California: a history of punk and new wave. Last Gasp of San Francisco. '83.

Belz, Carl. The story of rock. Oxford University Press. '72.

Betrock, Alan. Girl groups: the story of a sound. Delilah Books. '82.

Blair, John. The illustrated discography of surf music, 1961–1965. Pieran Press. '85. (rev. ed.)

Bockris, Victor and Malanga, Gerard. Up-tight: the Velvet Underground story. Omnibus Press. '83.

Boot, Adrian and Thomas, Michael. Jamaica: Babylon on thin wire. Thames and Hudson. '76.

Brown, Charles T. The art of rock and roll. Prentice-Hall. '87. (rev. ed.)

Brown, Charles T. The rock and roll story: from the sounds of rebellion to an American art form. Prentice-Hall. '83.

Brown, Peter and Gaines, Steven. The love you make: an inside story of the Beatles. Macmillan. '83.

Burchill, Julie and Parsons, Tony. The boy looked at Johnny: the obituary of rock and roll. Pluto Press. '78.

Burston, Jeremy. Led Zeppelin: the book. Proteus. '82.

Carr, Roy. David Bowie: an illustrated record. Eel Pie. '81.

Christgau, Robert. Any old way you choose it: rock and other pop music 1967-1973. Penguin Books. '73.

*Clark, Al, ed. Rock yearbook 1983. St. Martin's Press. '83.

Clarke, Sebastion. Jah music. Heinemann Educational. '80.

Cohn, Nik. Awopbopaloobopalopbamboom: pop from the beginning. Paladin. '72. (rev. ed.)

Connolly, Ray. John Lennon 1940-1980. Fontana Paperbacks. '81.

Coon, Caroline. 1988: the new wave punk rock explosion. Hawthorn Books. '77.

Coryell, Julie. Jazz-rock fusion: the people, the music. Marion Boyars. '78.

Cotton, Jonathan and Doudna, Christine, eds. The ballad of John and Yoko. Doubleday. '82.

Damsker, Matt, ed. Rock voices: the best lyrics of an era. St. Martin's Press. '80.

Davis, Stephen. Bob Marley: the biography. Arthur Barker. '83.

Davis, Stephen and Simon, Peter. Reggae international. Thames and Hudson. '83.

Denisoff, R. Serge. Sing a song of social significance. Bowling Green University Press. '72.

Denisoff, R. Serge and Peterson, Richard A. The sounds of social change: studies in popular culture. Rand McNally. '72.

Dewitt, Howard A. Chuck Berry: rock 'n' roll music. Horizon Books. '81.

Duncan, R. The noise: notes from a rock 'n' roll era. Ticknor & Fields. '84.

Eisen, Jonathan. Altamont: death of innocence in the Woodstock generation. Avon. '70.

Eisen, Jonathan, ed. The age of rock: sounds of the American cultural revolution, a reader. Vintage Books. '69.

Elson, Howard. Early rockers. Proteus. '82.

*Ferris, William and Hart, Mary L., eds. Folk music and modern sound. University Press of Mississippi. '82.

Flanagan, Bill. Written in my soul: rock's great songwriters talk about creating their own music. Contemporary Books. '86.

Fletcher, Peter. Roll over rock: a study of music in contemporary culture. Stainer & Bell. '81.

Friedman, Myra. Buried alive: a biography of Janis Joplin. Morrow. '73.

Frith, Simon. The sociology of rock. Constable. '78.

Frith, Simon. Sound effects: youth, leisure, and the politics of rock. Constable. '83. (rev. ed.)

Frith, Simon. Sound effects: youth, leisure, and the politics of rock 'n' roll. Pantheon. '81.

Gambaccini, Paul. Masters of rock. Omnibus Press. '82.

Garcia, Jerry. Garcia: the Rolling Stone interview. Straight Arrow Books. '72.

Garland, Phyl. The sound of soul. Henry Regnery. '69.

Gill, Chris and Futtrell, Jon. The illustrated encyclopedia of black music. Salamander Books. '82.

Gillett, Charlie. The sound of the city: The rise of rock and roll. Pantheon. '84. (rev. ed.)

Gleason, Ralph J. The Jefferson Airplane and the San Francisco sound. Ballantine Books. '69.

Goldman, Albert. Elvis. McGraw-Hill. '81.

Goldrosen, John J. Buddy Holly: his life and music. Quick Fox. '79 (rev. ed.)

Goldstein, Richard. Goldstein's greatest hits: a book mostly about rock 'n' roll. Prentice-Hall. '70.

Guitar Player Magazine. Rock guitarists: from the pages of Guitar Player Magazine. Guitar Player Books. '75.

Guralnick, Peter. Feel like going home: portraits in blues & rock 'n' roll. Omnibus Press. '78.

Guralnick, Peter. Lost highway: journeys & arrivals of American musicians. David R. Godine. '79.

Haralambres, Michael. Right on: from blues to soul in black America. Da Capo Press. '79.

Harrison, Hank. The Grateful Dead. Flash Books. '75.

Harry, Debbie, Stein, Chris and Bockris, Victor. Making tracks: The rise of Blondie. Elm Tree Books. '82.

Haskins, James. The story of Stevie Wonder. Lothrop, Lee & Shepard. '76.

*Hemphill, Paul. The Nashville sound: bright lights and country music. Simon and Schuster. '70.

Henderson, Davis. 'Scuze me while I kiss the sky: the life of Jimi Hendrix. Bantam. '81.

Herbst, Peter, ed. The Rolling Stone interviews 1967-1980: talking with the legends of rock & roll. St. Martin's Press. '81.

Hoare, Ian, ed. The soul book. Eyre Methuen. '75.

Hopkins, Jerry. Elvis. Simon & Schuster. '71.

Hopkins, Jerry. Elvis: the final years. St. Martin's Press. '80.

Hopkins, Jerry. Festival!: the book of American music celebrations. Macmillan. '70.

Hopkins, Jerry. The rock story. Signet. '70.

Hopkins, Jerry and Sugerman, Daniel. No one here gets out alive. Warner Books. '80.

Humphries, Patrick. Bookends: the Simon and Garfunkel story. Proteus. '82.

Jahn, Mike. Jim Morrison and the Doors: An unauthorized book. Grosset & Dunlap. '69.

Jaspar, Tony and Oliver, Derek. The international encyclopedia of hard rock & heavy metal. Sidgwick & Jackson. '84.

Juby, Kerry. David Bowie. Midas Books. '82.

Klein, Joe. Woody Guthrie: a life. Faber. '81.

Knight, Curtis. Jimi: an intimate biography of Jimi Hendrix. Praeger. '74.

Kooper, Al. Backstage passes: rock'n'roll life in the sixties. '76.

Laing, Dave. Buddy Holly. Macmillan. '72.

Laing, Dave. One chord wonders: power and meaning in punk rock. Open University Press. '85.

Laing, Dave. The sound of our time. Sheed and Ward. '69.

Laing, Dave and Shelton, Robert. The electric muse: the story of folk into rock. Eyre Methuen. '75.

Landau, Jon. It's too late to stop now: a rock and roll journal. Straight Arrow Books. '72.

Leaf, David. The Beach Boys and the California myth. Grosset & Dunlap. '78.

Lennon, John. Lennon remembers: the Rolling Stone interviews. Straight Arrow Books. '71.

Lydon, Michael. Boogie lightnin'. Dial Press. '74.

Mabey, Richard. The pop process. Hutchinson Educational. '69.

Marcus, Greil. Mystery train: images of America in rock'n'roll music. Dutton. '82. (rev. ed.)

Marcus, Greil, ed. Rock and roll will stand. Beacon Press. '69.

Marcus, Griel, ed. Stranded: rock and roll for a desert island. Alfred A. Knopf. '79.

Marsh, Dave. Before I get old: the story of the Who. St. Martin's Press. '83.

Marsh, Dave. The book of rock lists. Dell. '81.

Marsh, Dave. Born to run: The Bruce Springsteen story. Dell. '81. (rev. ed.)

Marsh, Dave. Elvis. New York Times Books. '82.

*Marsh, Dave. The first rock and roll confidential report. Duke and Duchess Ventures, Inc./Pantheon Books. '85.

Marsh, Dave. Fortunate son: criticism and journalism by America's best-known rock writer. Random House. '85.

Marsh, Dave. Paul Simon. Quick Fox. '78.

Martin, George. All you need is ears. Macmillan. '79.

Mellers, Wilfrid. Twilight of the gods: The Beatles in retrospect. Faber. '76.

Middleton, Richard. Pop music and the blues: a study of the relationship and its significance. Gollancz. '72.

Miles, ed. The New Wave Encyclopedia. Omnibus Press. '81.

*Miller, Jim, ed. The Rolling Stone illustrated history of rock & roll. Rolling Stone Press/Random House. '76.

Miller, Jim, ed. The Rolling Stone illustrated history of rock. Random House. '81. (rev. ed.)

Nicholas, A.X., ed. The poetry of soul. Bantam Books. '71.

Nite, Norm N. and Crespo, Charles. Rock on: the illustrated encyclopedia of rock'n'roll. Harper & Row. '82. (rev. ed.)

Norman, Philip. The road goes on forever: portraits from a journey through contemporary music. Simon & Schuster. '82.

Norman, Philip. Shout!: the true story of the Beatles. Simon & Schuster. '82.

Norman, Philip. The Stones. Simon & Schuster. '84.

Orloff, Katherine. Rock'n'roll woman. Nash Publishing. '74.

Orman, John M. The politics of rock music. Nelson-Hall. '84.

Palmer, Myles. New wave explosion: how punk became new wave became the 80's. Proteus. '81.

Palmer, Robert. Baby, that was rock & roll: the legendary Leiber & Stoller. Harcourt Brace Jovanovich. '78.

Palmer, Robert. Jerry Lee Lewis. Omnibus Press. '81.

Pichaske, David. A generation in motown: popular music and culture in the sixties. Schirmer Books. '79.

Pidgeon, John. Eric Clapton: a biography. Panther. '76.

Pielke, Robert G. You say you want a revolution: rock music in American culture. Nelson-Hall. '86.

Pollock, Bruce. In their own words: lyrics and lyricists 1955–1974. Macmillan. '75.

Pollock, Bruce. When rock was young: a nostalgic review of the Top Forty era. Holt, Rinehart & Winston. '81.

Pollock, Bruce. When the music mattered: rock in the 1960's. Holt, Rinehart & Winston. '84.

*Pratt, Linda Ray. Elvis, or the ironies of a Southern identity. '79.

Price, Steven D. Take me home: the rise of country and western music. Praeger. '74.

Redd, Lawrence N. Rock is rhythm and blues: the impact of mass media. Michigan State University Press. '74.

Reese, Krista. Elvis Costello: completely false biography based on rumor, innuendo and lies. Proteus. '81.

Reese, Krista. The name of this book is Talking Heads. Proteus. '82.

Reid, Jan. The improbable rise of redneck rock. Da Capo Press. '77.

Reidel, Johannes. Soul music, black and white: the influence of black music on the churches. Augsberg Publishing House. '75.

Rimmer, Dave. Like punk never happened: Culture Club and the new pop. Faber and Faber. '85.

Rivelli, Pauline and Levin, Robert, eds. Giants of black music. Da Capo. '81.

Roach, Dusty. Patti Smith: rock & roll madonna. And Books. '79.

Rockwell, John. All American music: composition in late twentieth century. Alfred A. Knopf. '83.

Rogan, Johnny. Neil Young: the definitive story of his musical career. Proteus. '82.

Rogers, Dave. Rock 'n' roll. Routledge & Kegan Paul. '82.

The Rolling Stone interviews. Paperback Library. '71.

The Rolling Stone interviews: volume two. Warner Books. '73.

Rolling Stones, the. Our own story. Bantam Books. '70. (rev. ed.)

The Rolling Stones. Straight Arrow Books. '75.

Rowe, Mike. Chicago breakdown. Drake. '75.

Rowers, Barbara. Grace Slick: the biography. Doubleday. '80.

Roxon, Lillian and Naha, Ed. Lillian Roxon's rock encyclopedia. Grosset & Dunlap. '78. (rev. ed.)

Rublowsky, John. Black music. Basic Books. '71.

Russell, Ethan A. Dear Mr. Fantasy: diary of a decade; our time and rock and roll. Houghton Mifflin. '85.

Sanchez, Tony. Up and down with the Rolling Stones. William Morrow. '79.

Sander, Ellen. Trips: rock life in the sixties. Charles Scribner's Sons. '73.

Santelli, Robert. Aquarius rising: rock festival years. Dell. '80.

Sawyer, Charles. The arrival of B. B. King. Doubleday. '80.

Scaduto, Anthony. Bob Dylan. New American Library. '79. (rev. ed.)

Schafer, William John. Rock music: where it's been, what it means, where it's going. Augsberg Publishing House. '72.

Schaffner, Nicholas. The Beatles forever. McGraw-Hill. '78.

Schaffner, Nicholas. The boys from Liverpool: John, Paul, George, Ringo. Methuen. '80.

Schaffner, Nicholas. British invasion: from the first wave to the new wave. McGraw-Hill. '82.

Schaffner, Nicholas and Shotton, Pete. John Lennon: in my life. Stein & Day. '83.

Sculatti, Gene and Seay, Davin. San Francisco nights: the psychedelic music trip, 1965–1968. St. Martin's Press. '85.

Shaw, Arnold. The rockin' '50s: the decade that transformed the pop music scene. Hawthorn Books. '74.

Shaw, Arnold. The world of soul: black America's contribution to the pop music scene. Cowles Book Company. '70.

Shevey, Sandra. Ladies of pop-rock. Scholastic Book Service. '72.

Simels, Steven. Gender chameleons: androgyny in rock 'n' roll. Arbor House. '85.

Spitz, Robert Stephen. Barefoot in Babylon: the creation of the Woodstock music festival 1969. Viking Press. '79.

Statzmary, David P. Rockin' in time: a social history of rock and roll. Prentice-Hall. '87.

Street, John. Rebel rock: the politics of popular music. Blackwell. '86.

Swenson, John. The Eagles. Ace Books. '81.

Tharpe, Jac L. Elvis: images and fancies. University Press of Mississippi. '80.

Thompson, Toby. Positively Main Street: an unorthodox view of Bob Dylan. New English Library. '72.

Thomson, Liz. New women in rock. Omnibus Press. '82.

Tobler, John and Grundy, Stuart. The guitar greats. British Broadcasting Corporation. '83.

Too fast to live, too young to die. Plexus. '82.

Tosches, Nick. Hellfire: the Jerry Lee Lewis story. Delacorte. '82.

Tosches, Nick. Unsung heroes of rock 'n' roll. Charles Scribner's Sons. '84.

Tremlett, George. The David Bowie story. Warner Paperback Library. '75.

Tremlett, George. The Paul McCartney story. Futura Publications. '75.

Walley, David. No commercial potential: the saga of Frank Zappa then & now. Dutton. '80.

Ward, Ed, Stokes, Geoffrey and Tucker, Ken. Rock of ages: the Rolling Stone history of rock & roll. Rolling Stone Press. '86.

Weinberg, Max and Santelli, Robert. The big beat: conversations with rock's great drummers. Contemporary Books. '84.

*Whitcomb, Ian. Rock Odyssey. Doubleday. '83.

Williams, Paul. Outlaw blues: book of rock music. E. P. Dutton. '69.

Williams, Richard. Out of his head: the sound of Phil Spector. Dutton. '72.

Zimmer, Dave. Crosby, Stills & Nash: the authorized biography. St. Martin's Press. '84.

PERIODICALS

Little Richard: from A to Zeeza. Artforum. 23:80. D. '84.

Less than zero: Elvis Costello and the L.A. sign system. Artforum. 24:12. S. '85.

Elvis Costello: in the kingdom of the invisible. Artforum. 24:12. Mr. '86.

The changing face of pop: an inside look. Down Beat. 53:58+. F. '86.

*Back on the street again. Kit Rachlis. Mother Jones. 7:12+. Ja. '82.

*Some future. Jim Miller. New Republic. 108:25-8. Mr. 24, '79.

*They changed rock, which changed the culture, which changed us. Jeff Greenfield. New York Times Magazine. p12+. F. 16, '75.

Rock lives! J. Rockwell. New York Times Magazine. p61+. F. 27, '77.

Rock bottom: punk rock. Newsweek. 89:80+. Je. 20, '77.

Bang! It's the Sex Pistols. Newsweek. 91:71. Ja. 16, '78.

Return of the rock heroes. Newsweek. 103:100. Je. 18, '84.

Rock's new women. Newsweek. 105:48-54+. Mr. 4, '85.

He's on fire. Newsweek. 106:48-54. Ag. 5, '85.

All-American music. Newsweek. 108:62+. S. 8, '86.

*From 'race music' to heavy metal: a fiery history of protests. Steven Dougherty. People Weekly. 24:52+. S. 16, '85.

*The punk meets the godmother. Pete Townshend. Rolling Stone. p54+. N. 17, '77.

The Clash: anger on the left. Rolling Stone. p8+. Mr. 8, '79.

Prince. Rolling Stone. p18+. Ap. 28, '83.

London calling. Rolling Stone. p17+. N. 10, '83.

*Ad nauseam: how MTV sells out rock & roll. Steven Levy. Rolling Stone. p30+. D. 8, '83.

Bruce Springsteen (interview). Rolling Stone. p18-19+. D. 6, '84.

Bruce Springsteen: made in the U.S.A. Rolling Stone. p20+. O. 10, '85.

*The music that changed the world. Kurt Loder. Rolling Stone. p49-50. F. 13, '86.

Down to Old Dixie and back: The Band. Time. 95:42+. Ja. 12, '70.

Backstreet phantom of rock (Bruce Springsteen). Time. 106:48+. O. 27, '75.

These big girls don't cry. Time. 125:74-75. Mr. 4, '85.

Madonna rocks the land. Time. 125:74+. My. 27, '85.

'Round the world, a Boss boom. Time. 126:68-9+. Ag. 26, '85.

*Songs from the high ground. Jay Cocks and staff reporters. Time. 126:78+. O. 7, '85.

Rock's renaissance man: David Byrne. Time. 128:78+. S. '86.